Knit with DEBORAH NORVILLE

LEISURE ARTS, INC.
LITTLE ROCK, AR

EDITORIAL STAFF
Managing Editor: Susan White Sullivan
Knit and Crochet Director: Debra Nettles
Special Projects Director: Susan Frantz Wiles
Senior Prepress Director: Mark Hawkins
Technical Writer/Editor: Cathy Hardy
Contributing Editors: Linda Daley, Sarah J. Green, and Lois J. Long
Editorial Writers: Merrilee Gasaway and Susan McManus Johnson
Art Publications Director: Rhonda Shelby
Senior Graphic Artist: Lora Puls
Graphic Artists: Amy Temple, Dayle Carozza and Janie Wright
Photography Manager: Katherine Atchison
Photography Stylist: Angela Alexander
Photographer: Jason Masters

BUSINESS STAFF
Vice President and Chief Operations Officer: Tom Siebenmorgen
Director of Finance and Administration: Laticia Mull Dittrich
Vice President, Sales and Marketing: Pam Stebbins
National Accounts Director: Martha Adams
Sales and Services Director: Margaret Reinold
Controller: Francis Caple
Vice President, Operations: Jim Dittrich
Comptroller, Operations: Rob Thieme
Retail Customer Service Manager: Stan Raynor
Print Production Manager: Fred F. Pruss

Instructions tested and photo models made by JoAnn Bowling, Susan Carter, Lee Ellis, Sue Galucki, Raymelle Greening, Dale Potter, Margaret Taverner, and Ted Tomany.

Library of Congress Control Number: 2008942178

ISBN-13: 978-160140-997-3
ISBN-10: 1-60140-997-4

10 9 8 7 6 5 4 3 2 1

TABLE OF *Contents*

Deborah Norville ON KNITTING

I can't think of a time in my life when I didn't have a needle in my hand—or a pair of them. My love of needlearts began with those preprinted embroidery kits. I still have the dresser scarf I made when I was four or five years old! As a little girl, I was fascinated by the blur of my mother's knitting needles as she worked away, lulled by the comforting methodical click of her stitches. I'd sit mesmerized as I watched a unique garment grow with each successive row.

"Those aren't needles," I'd marvel. "They're magic wands!"

My own early efforts at knitting were disastrous. My small hands weren't coordinated enough to master it. But I persevered, and by the time I was eight years old, I got the hang of it. It was the beginning of miles of scarves, mountains of mittens, oodles of afghans, and—when I was feeling really

One of my greatest joys has been teaching my daughter, Mikaela, how to knit.

— Deborah

ambitious—the occasional sweater. And that was just the knitting. There were needlepoint pillows, crewel and cross stitch samplers, macramé, smocked tops and even hand-knotted rugs. I felt a smile with every stitch, and with each completed project my self-esteem grew.

But YOU never knew this. It wasn't something I could talk about while building a career as a television journalist. When your job requires a "tough as nails reporter" image, the network bosses don't encourage you to talk about the Christmas stocking you made. So I'd fly to Washington, interview the First Lady, and be sure I had my knitting hidden in my travel bag!

That was then. Now I kill down-time on the set by working on my latest project. I've led my colleagues at "Inside Edition" in knitting classes. We come into work a little early, gossip and knit a bit and then dive into the madness of doing a daily television show. I even got the boss to let me do a series on the joys of handmade gift giving.

For me, it's really about returning to my roots. Textiles run in my blood. My hometown of Dalton, Georgia is the "carpet capital of the world." One of my dad's early businesses was spinning yarn for the carpet mills. My grandmother made and sold chenille bedspreads during the Depression. So when Premier Yarns approached me about partnering to create the Deborah Norville Collection, I felt life was coming full circle.

Finally, I was returning to the textile business of my family.

The new yarn is called "Serenity" because knitting brings such a welcome calm. This book is designed to help you start or continue your own tradition of relaxing with knitting.

If you are making a gift for someone else or indulging in a present for yourself, the range of projects I've chosen for this book will have something that's right for you.

Need instant gratification? Try the cool media holders or the baby booties. Feeling ambitious? Check out the openwork pillows shown on pages 6 and 8. They're actually a repeat of the patterns of the afghan on page 7. The stitches look tricky—but they aren't! Want your kids or partner to think of you when you're not there? Knit them one of the great toboggan hats on page 37. They will be sure to think of you each time they pull it on, just as you thought of them while you were knitting. There's a reason my tagline is "A Smile In Every Stitch!"

So pull out your needles, pick out a project and start knitting away. See if you don't find a smile in every one of your stitches. And be sure to let me know how it goes! Go to www.dnorville.com and send me an e-mail —and be sure to check out the knitting corner while you're there.

See if you don't find a smile in every one of your stitches.

afghan & pillow

◼◼◼◻ **INTERMEDIATE**

Finished Sizes
Afghan: 42½" x 56" (108 cm x 142 cm)
Pillow: 14" (35.5 cm) square

MATERIALS

Deborah Norville Collection, Serenity Worsted Weight Yarn
  [3.5 ounces, 186 yards (100 grams, 170 meters) per skein]:
    #08 Grenadine
    Afghan - 12 skeins
    Pillow - 3 skeins
31" (78.5 cm) Circular knitting needle, size 15 (10 mm) **or**
  size needed for gauge
Pillow form - 14" (35.5 cm) square
Fabric for pillow lining (optional) - 18½" x 36" (45.5 cm x 91.5 cm)
Yarn needle

♦ **GAUGE:** Holding 2 strands together, in Stockinette Stitch,
       11 sts and 14 rows = 4" (10 cm)

AFGHAN

Holding 2 strands together, cast on 106 sts.

Row 1: (K1, P1) across.

Row 2 (Right side)**:** (P1, K1) across.

Rows 3-9: Repeat Rows 1 and 2, 3 times; then repeat Row 1 once **more**.

This cozy afghan and pillow set is surprisingly quick to knit by holding two strands of Serenity Worsted Weight Yarn together and using large needles. The fun mix of textures will work well with any décor.

Pillow Front

Instructions continue on page 8.

*Repeat after me: **I can do this**! And you can, too! This exquisite afghan is really just two simple patterns combined with a seed stitch border. If you're like me, you'll make one of these and then decide you need one for every room in the house.*

—Deborah

Row 10: P1, (K1, P1) 3 times, K2, YO *(Fig. 3a, page 73)*, K1, YO, K2 tog *(Fig. 8, page 75)*, K5, YO, K1, YO, K2 tog, ★ K 25, YO, K1, YO, K2 tog, K5, YO, K1, YO, K2 tog; repeat from ★ once **more**, K8, (P1, K1) 3 times: 112 sts.

Row 11: K1, (P1, K1) 3 times, P6, P2 tog *(Fig. 11, page 76)*, P7, P2 tog, ★ P 27, P2 tog, P7, P2 tog; repeat from ★ once **more**, P6, (K1, P1) 3 times: 106 sts.

Row 12: P1, (K1, P1) 3 times, K2, YO, K1, YO, K2, K2 tog, K3, YO, K1, YO, K2, K2 tog, ★ K 23, YO, K1, YO, K2, K2 tog, K3, YO, K1, YO, K2, K2 tog; repeat from ★ once **more**, K6, (P1, K1) 3 times: 112 sts.

Row 13: K1, (P1, K1) 3 times, P4, P2 tog, P7, P2 tog, ★ P 27, P2 tog, P7, P2 tog; repeat from ★ once **more**, P8, (K1, P1) 3 times: 106 sts.

Row 14: P1, (K1, P1) 3 times, K3, YO, K4, K2 tog, (K1, YO) twice, K4, K2 tog, K1, YO, ★ K 21, YO, K4, K2 tog, (K1, YO) twice, K4, K2 tog, K1, YO; repeat from ★ once **more**, K3, (P1, K1) 3 times: 112 sts.

Row 15: K1, (P1, K1) 3 times, P3, P2 tog, P7, P2 tog, ★ P 27, P2 tog, P7, P2 tog; repeat from ★ once **more**, P9, (K1, P1) 3 times: 106 sts.

Row 16: P1, (K1, P1) 3 times, K7, K2 tog, YO, K1, YO, K5, K2 tog, YO, K1, YO, ★ K 25, K2 tog, YO, K1, YO, K5, K2 tog, YO, K1, YO; repeat from ★ once **more**, K3, (P1, K1) 3 times: 112 sts.

Row 17: K1, (P1, K1) 3 times, P5, P2 tog, P7, P2 tog, ★ P 27, P2 tog, P7, P2 tog; repeat from ★ once **more**, P7, (K1, P1) 3 times: 106 sts.

Row 18: P1, (K1, P1) 3 times, K5, K2 tog, K2, YO, K1, YO, K3, K2 tog, K2, YO, K1, YO, ★ K 23, K2 tog, K2, YO, K1, YO, K3, K2 tog, K2, YO, K1, YO; repeat from ★ once **more**, K3, (P1, K1) 3 times: 112 sts.

Row 19: K1, (P1, K1) 3 times, (P7, P2 tog) twice, ★ P4, K 16, (P7, P2 tog) twice; repeat from ★ once **more**, P5, (K1, P1) 3 times: 106 sts.

Row 20: P1, (K1, P1) 3 times, † K2, YO, K1, K2 tog, K4, (YO, K1) twice, K2 tog, K4, YO †, ★ K3, (YO, P2 tog) 8 times *(Figs. 3b & c, page 73)*, repeat from † to † once; repeat from ★ once **more**, K4, (P1, K1) 3 times: 112 sts.

Row 21: K1, (P1, K1) 3 times, P8, P2 tog, P7, P2 tog, ★ P3, K 16, P8, P2 tog, P7, P2 tog; repeat from ★ once **more**, P4, (K1, P1) 3 times: 106 sts.

Pillow Back

Repeat Rows 10-21 for pattern until Afghan measures approximately 54" (137 cm) from cast on edge, ending by working Row 17: 106 sts.

Next Row: (P1, K1) across.

Next Row: (K1, P1) across.

Next Row: (P1, K1) across.

Repeat last 2 rows, 3 times.

Bind off all sts in pattern.

PILLOW
BACK
Holding 2 strands together, cast on 36 sts.

Row 1 (Right side)**:** Knit across.

Row 2: Purl across.

Rows 3-8: Repeat Rows 1 and 2, 3 times.

Rows 9 and 10: Knit across.

Row 11 (Eyelet row)**:** K1, (P2 tog, YO) across to last st *(Fig. 11, page 76 and Figs. 3b & d, page 73)*, K1.

Rows 12 and 13: Knit across.

Rows 14-57: Repeat Rows 2-13, 3 times; then repeat Rows 2-9 once **more**.

Bind off all sts in **purl**.

FRONT
Holding 2 strands together, cast on 36 sts.

Row 1: Purl across.

Row 2 (Right side)**:** K2, YO *(Fig. 3a, page 73)*, K1, YO, K2 tog *(Fig. 8, page 75)*, ★ K5, YO, K1, YO, K2 tog; repeat from ★ across to last 7 sts, K7: 40 sts.

Row 3: P6, P2 tog, (P7, P2 tog) across to last 5 sts, P5: 36 sts.

Row 4: K2, YO, K1, YO, K2, K2 tog, ★ K3, YO, K1, YO, K2, K2 tog; repeat from ★ across to last 5 sts, K5: 40 sts.

Row 5: P4, (P2 tog, P7) across: 36 sts.

Row 6: K3, YO, K4, K2 tog, ★ (K1, YO) twice, K4, K2 tog; repeat from ★ across to last 3 sts, K1, YO, K2: 40 sts.

Row 7: P3, P2 tog, (P7, P2 tog) across to last 8 sts, P8: 36 sts.

Row 8: K7, K2 tog, YO, K1, YO, ★ K5, K2 tog, YO, K1, YO; repeat from ★ across to last 2 sts, K2: 40 sts.

Row 9: P5, P2 tog, (P7, P2 tog) across to last 6 sts, P6: 36 sts.

Row 10: K5, K2 tog, K2, YO, K1, YO, ★ K3, K2 tog, K2, YO, K1, YO; repeat from ★ across to last 2 sts, K2: 40 sts.

Row 11: (P7, P2 tog) across to last 4 sts, P4: 36 sts.

Row 12: K2, YO, K1, K2 tog, K4, ★ (YO, K1) twice, K2 tog, K4; repeat from ★ across to last 3 sts, YO, K3: 40 sts.

Row 13: P8, P2 tog, (P7, P2 tog) across to last 3 sts, P3: 36 sts.

Rows 14-57: Repeat Rows 2-13, 3 times; then repeat Rows 2-9 once **more**: 36 sts.

Row 58: Knit across.

Bind off all sts in **purl**.

Cover pillow form if desired.

Using one strand, sew Front and Back together, inserting pillow form before closing.

Designs by Lee Tribett.

hoodie

Size	Finished Chest Measurement
12	32" (81.5 cm)
14	33½" (85 cm)
32	35½" (90 cm)
34	37" (94 cm)
36	39" (99 cm)
38	41" (104 cm)

Size Note: Instructions are written with sizes 12, 14, and 32 in the first set of braces { } and sizes 34, 36, and 38 in the second set of braces. Instructions will be easier to read if you circle all the numbers pertaining to your size. If only one number is given, it applies to all sizes.

Thrill someone with a hoodie knitted in their favorite color! You can also add a second color on the ribbings and drawstring casing. This pattern is unisex, and the classic styling is perfect for teens or adults!

MATERIALS

Deborah Norville Collection, Serenity Worsted Weight Yarn **MEDIUM 4**
  [3.5 ounces, 186 yards (100 grams, 170 meters) per skein]:
  Solid
  #51 Dark Shadow - {5-6-6}{7-7-8} skeins
  Two Colors
  Main Color #20 Hyacinth - {4-5-5}{6-6-7} skeins
  Contrasting Color #48 Heather Grey - {1-1-2}{2-2-2} skein(s)
Straight knitting needles, sizes 7 (4.5 mm) **and** 9 (5.5 mm) **or** sizes
  needed for gauge
Stitch holder
Marker
Separating zipper - {18-20-22}{22-24-24}"/{45.5-51-56}{56-61-61} cm
Sewing needle and matching thread
Yarn needle

♦**GAUGE:** With larger size needles, in Stockinette Stitch,
      18 sts and 23 rows = 4" (10 cm)

Hoodie can be worked in one or two colors. Work the Ribbings and Casing with a contrasting color if desired.

Instructions continue on page 12.

I love these hoodies! They add just the right amount of warmth for a crisp fall day or when a spring evening turns off cool. Pair them with jeans, and they become all-around weekend favorites.

—Deborah

BACK
RIBBING

Using smaller size needles and Contrasting Color if desired, cast on {74-78-82}{86-90-94} sts.

Rows 1-4: (K1, P1) across.

Rows 5-8: (P1, K1) across.

Rows 9-12: (K1, P1) across.

BODY

Change to larger size needles and Main Color.

Beginning with a **knit** row, work in Stockinette Stitch (knit one row, purl one row) until Back measures approximately {12½-13½-15}{15¼-16-16½}"/ {32-34.5-38}{38.5-40.5-42} cm from cast on edge, ending by working a **purl** row.

ARMHOLE SHAPING
Rows 1 and 2: Bind off {4-4-5}{5-5-5} sts, work across: {66-70-72}{76-80-84} sts.

Row 3 (Decrease row)**:** K1, SSK **(Figs. 9a-c, page 75)**, knit across to last 3 sts, K2 tog **(Fig. 8, page 75)**, K1: {64-68-70} {74-78-82} sts.

Row 4 (Decrease row)**:** P1, P2 tog **(Fig. 11, page 76)**, purl across to last 3 sts, SSP **(Fig. 12, page 76)**, P1: {62-66-68}{72-76-80} sts.

Continue to decrease one stitch at **each** Armhole edge, every row, {1-2-2}{2-2-2} time(s) **more**; then decrease every other row, 3 times: {54-56-58}{62-66-70} sts.

Work even until Armholes measure approximately {7½-7¾-8½}{8¾-9-9½}"/ {19-19.5-21.5}{22-23-24} cm, ending by working a **purl** row.

SHOULDER SHAPING
Rows 1-4: Bind off {5-6-6} {6-6-7} sts, work across: {34-32-34}{38-42-42} sts.

Rows 5 and 6: Bind off {6-5-5}{7-7-6} sts, work across: {22-22-24}{24-28-30} sts.

Slip remaining sts onto st holder; cut yarn.

LEFT FRONT
RIBBING

Using smaller size needles and Contrasting Color if desired, cast on {36-38-40}{42-44-46} sts.

Row 1 (Right side)**:** (K1, P1) across to last 2 sts, K2.

Row 2: P2, (K1, P1) across.

Rows 3 and 4: Repeat Rows 1 and 2.

Rows 5-8: (P1, K1) across.

Rows 9-12: Repeat Rows 1 and 2 twice.

BODY

Change to larger size needles and Main Color.

Row 1: Knit across to last 6 sts, (P1, K1) 3 times (Band).

Row 2: (P1, K1) 3 times, purl across.

Rows 3 and 4: Repeat Rows 1 and 2.

Row 5: Knit across to last 5 sts, P1, K1, P1, K2.

Row 6: P2, K1, P1, K1, purl across.

Rows 7 and 8: Repeat Rows 5 and 6.

Repeat Rows 1-8 for pattern until Left Front measures same as Back to Armhole Shaping, ending by working a **wrong** side row.

ARMHOLE SHAPING

Maintain established pattern throughout.

Row 1: Bind off {4-4-5}{5-5-5} sts, work across: {32-34-35} {37-39-41} sts.

Row 2: Work across.

Row 3 (Decrease row): K1, SSK, work across: {31-33-34} {36-38-40} sts.

Row 4 (Decrease row): Work across to last 3 sts, SSP, P1: {30-32-33}{35-37-39} sts.

Continue to decrease one stitch at Armhole edge, every row, {1-2-2}{2-2-2} time(s) **more**; then decrease every other row, 3 times: {26-27-28}{30-32-34} sts.

Work even until Armhole measures approximately {5¹/₂-5³/₄-6¹/₂}{6³/₄-7-7¹/₂}"/ {14-14.5-16.5}{17-18-19} cm, ending by working a **right** side row.

NECK SHAPING

Row 1: Bind off {6-6-6}{6-7-8} sts, purl across: {20-21-22} {24-25-26} sts.

Row 2 (Decrease row): Knit across to last 3 sts, K2 tog, K1: {19-20-21}{23-24-25} sts.

Row 3 (Decrease row): P1, P2 tog, purl across: {18-19-20} {22-23-24} sts.

Instructions continue on page 14.

Note: Sweater width includes 2 edge stitches.

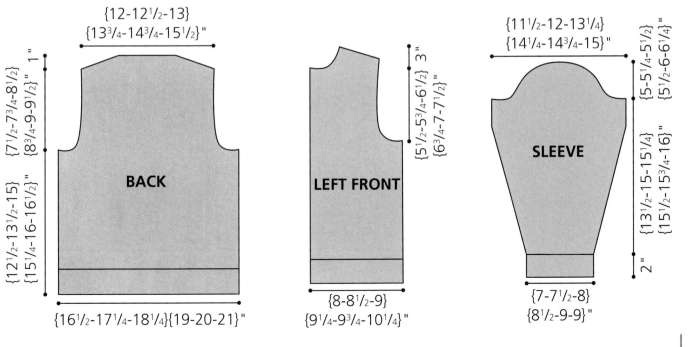

Row 4 (Decrease row)**:** Knit across to last 3 sts, K2 tog, K1: {17-18-19}{21-22-23} sts.

Row 5: Purl across.

Repeat Rows 4 and 5, {1-1-2}{2-3-3} time(s): {16-17-17}{19-19-20} sts.

Work even until Left Front measures same as Back to Shoulder Shaping, ending by working a **purl** row.

SHOULDER SHAPING
Row 1: Bind off {5-6-6}{6-6-7} sts, knit across: {11-11-11} {13-13-13} sts.

Row 2: Purl across.

Rows 3 and 4: Repeat Rows 1 and 2: {6-5-5}{7-7-6} sts.

Bind off remaining sts leaving a long end for sewing.

RIGHT FRONT
RIBBING
Using smaller size needles and Contrasting Color if desired, cast on {36-38-40}{42-44-46} sts.

Rows 1-4: (K1, P1) across.

Row 5 (Right side)**:** K2, (P1, K1) across.

Row 6: (P1, K1) across to last 2 sts, P2.

Rows 7 and 8: Repeat Rows 5 and 6.

Rows 9-12: (K1, P1) across.

BODY
Change to larger size needles and Main Color.

Row 1: K2, P1, K1, P1, knit across.

Row 2: Purl across to last 5 sts, K1, P1, K1, P2.

Rows 3 and 4: Repeat Rows 1 and 2.

Row 5: (K1, P1) 3 times (Band), knit across.

Row 6: Purl across to last 6 sts, (K1, P1) 3 times.

Rows 7 and 8: Repeat Rows 5 and 6.

Repeat Rows 1-8 for pattern unt Right Front measures same as Back to Armhole Shaping, endin by working a **right** side row.

ARMHOLE SHAPING
Maintain established pattern throughout.

Row 1: Bind off {4-4-5}{5-5-5} sts, work across: {32-34-35} {37-39-41} sts.

Row 2 (Decrease row)**:** Work across to last 3 sts, K2 tog, K1: {31-33-34}{36-38-40} sts.

Row 3 (Decrease row)**:** P1, P2 tog, work across: {30-32-33}{35-37-39} sts.

Continue to decrease one stitch at Armhole edge, every row, 1-2-2}{2-2-2} time(s) **more**; then decrease every other row, 3 times: {26-27-28}{30-32-34} sts.

Work even until Armhole measures same as Left Front to Neck Shaping, ending by working a **wrong** side row.

NECK SHAPING
Row 1: Bind off {6-6-6}{6-7-8} sts, knit across: {20-21-22} {24-25-26} sts.

Row 2: Purl across.

Row 3 (Decrease row)**:** K1, SSK, knit across: {19-20-21}{23-24-25} sts.

Row 4 (Decrease row)**:** Purl across to last 3 sts, SSP, P1: {18-19-20}{22-23-24} sts.

Row 5 (Decrease row)**:** K1, SSK, knit across: {17-18-19}{21-22-23} sts.

Row 6: Purl across.

Repeat Rows 5 and 6, {1-1-2}{2-3-3} time(s): {16-17-17}{19-19-20} sts.

Work even until Right Front measures same as Back to Shoulder Shaping, ending by working a **knit** row.

SHOULDER SHAPING
Row 1: Bind off {5-6-6}{6-6-7} sts, purl across: {11-11-11} {13-13-13} sts.

Row 2: Knit across.

Rows 3 and 4: Repeat Rows 1 and 2: {6-5-5}{7-7-6} sts.

Bind off remaining sts leaving a long end for sewing.

SLEEVE (Make 2)
RIBBING
Using smaller size needles and Contrasting Color if desired, cast on {32-34-36}{38-40-40} sts.

Rows 1-4: (K1, P1) across.

Rows 5-8: (P1, K1) across.

Rows 9-12: (K1, P1) across.

BODY
Change to larger size needles and Main Color.

Row 1 (Right side)**:** Knit across increasing 4 sts evenly spaced **(Fig. 6, page 74)**: {36-38-40} {42-44-44} sts.

Beginning with a **purl** row, work 5 rows in Stockinette Stitch.

Increase Row: K1, work right invisible increase, knit across to last st, work left invisible increase **(Figs. 7a & b, page 75)**, K1: {38-40-42}{44-46-46} sts.

Working in Stockinette Stitch, increase one stitch at **each** edge, every sixth row, {0-0-1}{5-4-7} time(s) **more (see Zeros, page 71)**; then increase every eighth row, {5-1-8}{5-6-4} time(s); then increase every tenth row, {2-6-0}{0-0-0} times: {52-54-60} {64-66-68} sts.

Work even until Sleeve measures approximately {15¹/₂-17-17¹/₄} {17¹/₂-17³/₄-18}"/{39.5-43-44} {44.5-45-45.5} cm from cast on edge, ending by working a **purl** row.

CAP SHAPING
Rows 1 and 2: Bind off {4-4-5}{5-5-5} sts, work across: {44-46-50}{54-56-58} sts.

Row 3 (Decrease row)**:** K1, SSK, knit across to last 3 sts, K2 tog, K1: {42-44-48}{52-54-56} sts.

Row 4: Purl across.

Repeat Rows 3 and 4, {10-11-12} {12-13-14} times **more**: {22-22-24}{28-28-28} sts.

Next 4 Rows: Bind off 4 sts, work across: {6-6-8}{12-12-12} sts.

Bind off remaining sts in **knit**.

Instructions continue on page 16.

FINISHING

Using long yarn ends, sew shoulder seams.

HOOD

With **right** side facing, using smaller size needles and Contrasting Color if desired, and beginning after 6 Band sts, pick up {16-16-16}{16-18-18} sts evenly spaced along Right Front Neck edge **(Figs. 17a & b, page 79)**, slip {22-22-24}{24-28-30} sts from Back st holder onto empty needle and knit across, pick up {16-16-16}{16-18-18} sts evenly spaced along Left Front Neck edge to Band: {54-54-56}{56-64-66} sts.

Row 1: K2, (P1, K1) across.

Row 2: (P1, K1) across to last 2 sts, P2.

Rows 3 and 4: Repeat Rows 1 and 2.

Row 5: (K1, P1) across to last 2 sts, K2.

Row 6: P2, (K1, P1) across.

Rows 7 and 8: Repeat Rows 5 and 6.

BOTTOM SHAPING

Change to larger size needle and Main Color.

Row 1: Purl across.

Row 2 (Increase row)**:** Knit {26-26-27}{27-31-32} sts, place marker **(see Markers, page 70)**, K1, work right invisible increase, knit across: {55-55-57}{57-65-67} sts.

Row 3: Purl across.

Row 4 (Increase row)**:** Knit across to marker, work right invisible increase, slip marker, K3, work left invisible increase, knit across: {57-57-59}{59-67-69} sts.

Rows 5-20: Repeat Rows 3 and 4, 8 times: {73-73-75}{75-83-85} sts.

Remove marker.

Work even until Hood measures approximately 12¼" (31 cm), ending by working a **purl** row.

TOP SHAPING

Row 1 (Decrease row)**:** Knit {34-34-35}{35-39-40} sts, K2 tog, place marker, K1, SSK, knit across: {71-71-73}{73-81-83} sts.

Row 2 (Decrease row)**:** Purl across to within 3 sts of marker, SSP, P1, P2 tog, purl across: {69-69-71}{71-79-81} sts.

Row 3 (Decrease row)**:** Knit across to within 2 sts of marker, K2 tog, K1, SSK, knit across: {67-67-69}{69-77-79} sts.

Rows 4-9: Repeat Rows 2 and 3, 3 times: {55-55-57}{57-65-67} sts.

Bind off all sts in **purl** leaving a long end for sewing.

Fold top of Hood in half and join bound off sts to form seam **(Figs. 16a & b, page 78)**.

CASING

With **right** side facing, using smaller size needles and Contrasting Color if desired, pick up 125 sts evenly spaced across Hood.

Row 1: K1, (P1, K1) across.

Row 2: P1, (K1, P1) across.

Row 3: K1, (P1, K1) across.

Rows 4-9: Repeat Rows 2 and 3, 3 times.

Bind off all sts in ribbing leaving a long end for sewing.

TWISTED CORD TIE

Using Contrasting Color if desired, make a Twisted Cord 40" (101.5 cm) long **or** to desired length **(see Twisted Cord, page 79)**.

Fold Hood Casing in half to **wrong** side, placing Tie inside, and sew bound off edge to picked up edge; sew end of rows of inside edge of Casing to Front Bands.

Sew Sleeves to Hoodie, placing center of last row on Sleeve Cap at shoulder seam and matching bound off stitches.

Weave underarm and side in one continuous seam **(Fig. 15, page 78)**.

Sew zipper in place, adjusting top of zipper as needed.

Design by Cathy Hardy.

Knit them short or knit them tall—this pattern makes both golf socks and crew socks. Serenity Sock Weight Yarn offers lots of fun variegated colors.

◼◼◼◻ **INTERMEDIATE**

Adult Size	Finished Ankle & Foot Circumference
Small	7½" (19 cm)
Medium	8" (20.5 cm)
Large	8½" (21.5 cm)

Size Note: Instructions are written for size Small with sizes Medium and Large in braces { }. Instructions will be easier to read if you circle all the numbers pertaining to your size. If only one number is given, it applies to all sizes.

We have this yarn in so many different colorways, every time you knit up these socks, you'll have something special!

— Deborah

MATERIALS

Deborah Norville Collection, Serenity Sock Weight Yarn **SUPER FINE 1**
[1.76 ounces, 230 yards (50 grams, 210 meters) per skein]:
   Golf #04-01 Tyme - 1 skein
   Crew #08-07 Citrine - 2 skeins
Set of 5 double pointed knitting needles, size 3 (3.25 mm)
   or size needed for gauge
Stitch holders - 2
Split-ring markers
Tapestry needle

Instructions continue on page 18.

Intimidated by the idea of making socks? Start with these golf socks! A few rows of ribbing at the ankle and you're ready to start the foot!

— Deborah

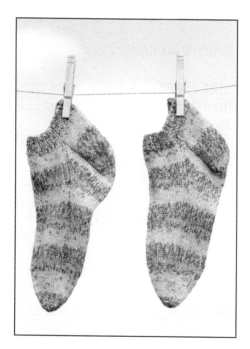

◆**GAUGE:** In Stockinette Stitch, 28 sts and 38 rows = 4" (10 cm)

When instructed to slip a stitch, always slip as if to **purl** with yarn held to **wrong** side, unless otherwise instructed.

LEG
Cast on 52{56-60} sts.

Slip 13{14-15} sts onto each of 3 double pointed needles, leaving 13{14-15} sts on the fourth needle *(see Using Double Pointed Needles, page 72)*.

The yarn end indicates the beginning of the round.

Rnd 1: (K3, P1) around.

Rnd 2: K1, P1, (K3, P1) around to last 2 sts, K2.

Golf
Repeat Rnds 1 and 2 for Seed ribbing until Leg measures approximately 1"(2.5 cm) from cast on edge.

Knit 2 rounds (Stockinette Stitch).

Crew
Repeat Rnds 1 and 2 for Seed ribbing until Leg measures approximately 5½{6-6½}"/ 14{15-16.5} cm from cast on edge **or** 1" (2.5 cm) less than desired length to Heel.

Knit every round (Stockinette Stitch) for 1" (2.5 cm).

HEEL
Dividing Stitches: Knit across first needle; slip sts from the next 2 needles onto 2 separate st holders for Instep to be worked later; **turn.**

HEEL FLAP
Row 1: Slip 1, P 25{27-29} all onto same needle.

The Heel Flap will be worked back and forth on two needles across these 26{28-30} sts.

Row 2: Slip 1, knit across.

Row 3: Slip 1, purl across.

Rows 4 thru 25{27-29}: Repeat Rows 2 and 3, 11{12-13} times.

TURNING HEEL

Begin working short rows as follows:

Row 1: Slip 1, K 16{18-20}, K2 tog **(Fig. 8, page 75)**, K1, leave remaining 6 sts unworked; **turn**.

Row 2: Slip 1, P9{11-13}, SSP **(Fig. 12, page 76)**, P1, leave remaining 6 sts unworked; turn.

Row 3: Slip 1, K 10{12-14}, K2 tog, K1, leave remaining 4 sts unworked; turn.

Row 4: Slip 1, P 11{13-15}, SSP, P1, leave remaining 4 sts unworked; turn.

Row 5: Slip 1, K 12{14-16}, K2 tog, K1, leave remaining 2 sts unworked; turn.

Row 6: Slip 1, P 13{15-17}, SSP, P1, leave remaining 2 sts unworked; turn.

Row 7: Slip 1, K 14{16-18}, K2 tog, K1.

Row 8: Slip 1, P 15{17-19}, SSP, P1: 18{20-22} sts remaining on needle; do **not** cut yarn.

GUSSET

The remainder of the sock will be worked in rounds.

Slip the Instep sts from the st holders onto 2 double pointed needles, 13{14-15} sts each.

FOUNDATION ROUND

With **right** side of Heel facing, using an empty double pointed needle and continuing with the working yarn, knit 9{10-11} of the Heel sts.
Place a split-ring marker around the next st to indicate the beginning of the round. Using an empty double pointed needle (this will be needle 1), knit across the remaining 9{10-11} Heel sts. With the same needle, pick up and knit 12{13-14} sts along the side of the Heel Flap **(Fig. 17a, page 79)** and one st in the corner.
With separate needles, knit across the Instep sts (needles 2 and 3).
With an empty needle, pick up and knit one st in the corner and 12{13-14} sts along the side of the Heel Flap. With the same needle, knit 9{10-11} Heel sts.

Stitch count is 22{24-26} sts on the first needle, 13{14-15} sts each on the second and third needles, and 22{24-26} sts on fourth needle for a total of 70{76-82} sts.

GUSSET DECREASES

Rnd 1 (Decrease rnd)**:** Knit across to the last 3 sts on first needle, K2 tog, K1; knit across the second and third needles; on fourth needle, K1, SSK **(Figs. 9a-c, page 75)**, knit across: 68{74-80} sts.

Rnd 2: Knit around.

Rnds 3 thru 18{20-22}: Repeat Rnds 1 and 2, 8{9-10} times: 52{56-60} sts, 13{14-15} sts on **each** needle.

FOOT

Knit every round until Foot measures approximately 6¼{7½-8¾}"/16{19-22} cm from the back of the Heel **or** desired length to Toe.

TOE

Rnd 1: ★ K 11{5-13}, K2 tog; repeat from ★ around: 48{48-56} sts.

Rnds 2-4: Knit around.

SIZE LARGE ONLY
Rnd 5: (K5, K2 tog) 8 times: 48 sts.

Rnds 6-8: Knit around.

ALL SIZES
Decrease Rnd: (K4, K2 tog) 8 times: 40 sts.

Decrease 8 sts every fourth rnd, working one less st between decreases, 4 times **more**: 8 sts.

Cut yarn leaving a long end for sewing. Thread tapestry needle with end and slip remaining sts onto tapestry needle; gather tightly to close and secure end.

woman's turtleneck

◖■■◻ INTERMEDIATE

Size	Finished Bust Measurement	
30	31"	(78.5 cm)
32	33"	(84 cm)
34	35½"	(90 cm)
36	37"	(94 cm)
38	39"	(99 cm)
40	41"	(104 cm)

Size Note: Instructions are written with sizes 30, 32, and 34 in the first set of braces { } and sizes 36, 38, and 40 in the second set of braces. Instructions will be easier to read if you circle all the numbers pertaining to your size. If only one number is given, it applies to all sizes.

An indispensable classic for everyone's wardrobe, this pullover looks amazing in any color of Serenity Worsted Weight Yarn. We've included smaller sizes suitable for teens.

MATERIALS

Deborah Norville Collection, Serenity Worsted Weight Yarn 🄌4
   [3.5 ounces, 186 yards (100 grams, 170 meters) per skein]:
     #28 Little Boy Blue - {4-5-5}{6-6-6} skeins
Straight knitting needles, sizes 7 (4.5 mm) **and** 9 (5.5 mm) **or** sizes needed for gauge
16" (40.5 cm) Circular knitting needle, size 7 (4.5 mm)
Stitch holders - 2
Marker
Yarn needle

♦**GAUGE:** With larger size needles, in Stockinette Stitch,
        18 sts and 23 rows = 4" (10 cm)

Instructions continue on page 22

No pattern book is complete without a great turtleneck sweater, and when it's done up in this cozy yarn, you'll want to make more than one.

—Deborah

BACK
RIBBING
Using smaller size straight needles, cast on {72-76-82} {86-90-94} sts.

Work in K1, P1 ribbing for 2" (5 cm).

BODY
Change to larger size needles.

Work in Stockinette Stitch (knit one row, purl one row) until piece measures approximately {13-14-15}{15-15-15}"/ {33-35.5-38}{38-38-38} cm from cast on edge, ending by working a **purl** row.

ARMHOLE SHAPING
Rows 1 and 2: Bind off {4-4-5}{5-5-6} sts, work across: {64-68-72}{76-80-82} sts.

Row 3 (Decrease row)**:** K1, SSK *(Figs. 9a-c, page 75)*, knit across to last 3 sts, K2 tog *(Fig. 8, page 75)*, K1: {62-66-70} {74-78-80} sts.

Row 4 (Decrease row)**:** P1, P2 tog *(Fig. 11, page 76)*, purl across to last 3 sts, SSP *(Fig. 12, page 76)*, P1: {60-64-68}{72-76-78} sts.

Continue to decrease one stitch at **each** Armhole edge, every row, {1-1-2}{2-2-2} time(s) **more**; then decrease every other row, {2-3-3}{4-4-4} times: {54-56-58} {60-64-66} sts.

Work even until Armholes measure approximately {7¼-8¼-8½}{8¾-9-9¼}"/ {18.5-21-21.5}{22-23-23.5} cm, ending by working a **purl** row.

SHOULDER SHAPING
Rows 1-4: Bind {5-5-6}{6-6-6} sts, work across: {34-36-34}{36-40-42} sts.

Rows 5 and 6: Bind off {6-6-5}{5-7-7} sts, work across: {22-24-24}{26-26-28} sts.

Slip remaining sts onto st holder; cut yarn.

FRONT
Work same as Back until Armholes measure approximately {4¼-5¼-5½}{5¾-6-6¼}"/ {11-13.5-14}{14.5-15-16} cm, ending by working a **knit** row: {54-56-58}{60-64-66} sts.

NECK SHAPING
Both sides of Neck are worked at the same time, using separate yarn for **each** side.

Row 1: Purl {22-22-23} {23-25-25} sts, slip next {10-12-12}{14-14-16} sts onto st holder; with second yarn, purl across: {22-22-23}{23-25-25} sts **each** side.

Row 2 (Decrease row)**:** Knit across to within 3 sts of Neck edge, K2 tog, K1; with second yarn, K1, SSK, knit across: {21-21-22}{22-24-24} sts **each** side.

Row 3 (Decrease row)**:** Purl across to within 3 sts of Neck edge, SSP, P1; with second yarn, P1, P2 tog, purl across: {20-20-21}{21-23-23} sts **each** side.

Row 4 (Decrease row)**:** Knit across to within 3 sts of Neck edge, K2 tog, K1; with second yarn, K1, SSK, knit across: {19-19-20}{20-22-22} sts **each** side.

Row 5: Purl across; with second yarn, purl across.

Rows 6-11: Repeat Rows 4 and 5, 3 times: {16-16-17}{17-19-19} sts **each** side.

SHOULDER SHAPING
Rows 1-4: Bind off {5-5-6} {6-6-6} sts at Armhole edge, work across; with second yarn, work across: {6-6-5}{5-7-7} sts **each** side.

Row 5: Bind off remaining sts on first side leaving a long end for sewing; with second yarn, knit across.

Bind off remaining sts leaving a long end for sewing.

SLEEVE (Make 2)
RIBBING
Using smaller size straight needles, cast on {34-36-38}{40-40-42} sts.

Work in K1, P1 ribbing for 2½" (6.5 cm), increasing 4 sts evenly spaced across last row *(see Increases, pages 74 and 75)*: {38-40-42}{44-44-46} sts.

BODY

Change to larger size needles.

Work in Stockinette Stitch, increasing one stitch at each edge, every sixth row, {0-0-0}{0-1-5} time(s) (see Zeros, page 71); then increase every eighth row, {0-9-8}{7-9-6} times, then increase every tenth row, {7-0-1}{2-0-0} time(s): {52-58-60}{62-64-68} sts.

Work even until Sleeve measures approximately {17-17¼-17½} {17¾-18-18¼}"/{43-44-44.5} {45-45.5-46.5} cm from cast on edge **or** to desired length, ending by working a **purl** row.

SLEEVE CAP

Rows 1 and 2: Bind off {4-4-5}{5-5-6} sts, work across: {44-50-50}{52-54-56} sts.

Row 3 (Decrease row)**:** K1, SSK, knit across to last 3 sts, K2 tog, K1: {42-48-48}{50-52-54} sts.

Row 4: Purl across.

Repeat Rows 3 and 4, {9-12-12} {12-13-14} times: {24-24-24} {26-26-26} sts.

Next 4 Rows: Bind off 4 sts, work across: {8-8-8}{10-10-10} sts.

Bind off remaining sts in **knit**.

FINISHING

Using long ends, sew shoulder seams.

NECK RIBBING

With **right** side facing and using circular needle, pick up 23 sts evenly spaced along left Front Neck edge **(Fig. 17a, page 79)**, knit {10-12-12}{14-14-16} sts from Front st holder, pick up 23 sts evenly spaced along right Front Neck edge, slip {22-24-24} {26-26-28} sts from Back st holder onto second end of circular needle and knit across, place marker to mark beginning of rnd **(see Markers, page 70)**: {78-82-82}{86-86-90} sts.

Work in K1, P1 ribbing for 5" (12.5 cm) **or** until desired length.

Bind off all sts **loosely** in ribbing.

Sew Sleeves to Sweater, placing center of last row on Sleeve Cap at shoulder seam and matching bound off stitches.

Weave underarm and side in one continuous seam **(Fig. 15, page 78)**.

Note: Sweater width includes 2 edge stitches.

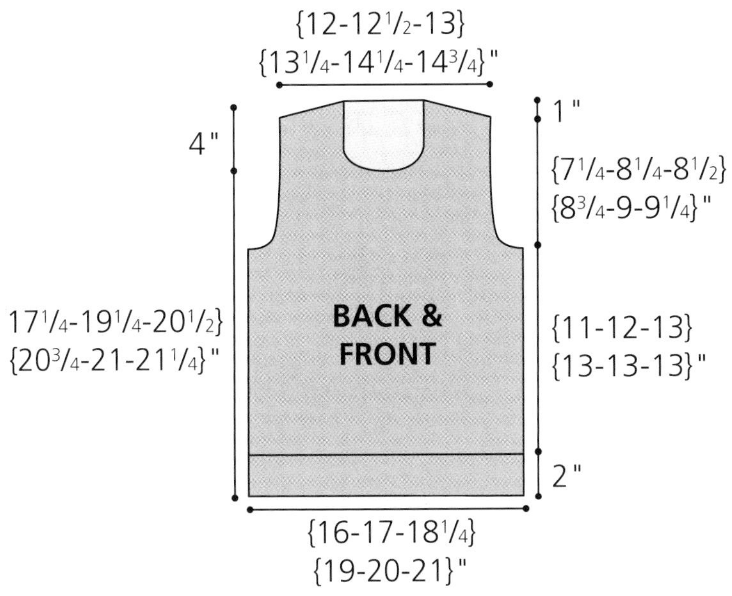

{12-12½-13}
{13¼-14¼-14¾}"

4"

1"

{7¼-8¼-8½}
{8¾-9-9¼}"

{17¼-19¼-20½}
{20¾-21-21¼}"

BACK & FRONT

{11-12-13}
{13-13-13}"

2"

{16-17-18¼}
{19-20-21}"

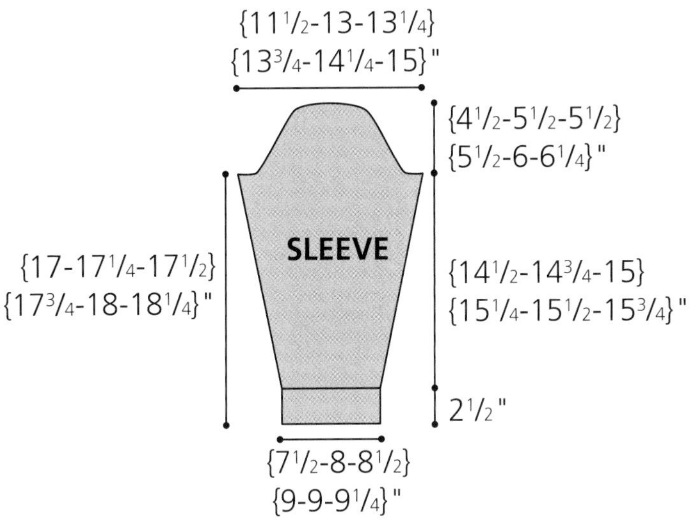

{11½-13-13¼}
{13¾-14¼-15}"

{4½-5½-5½}
{5½-6-6¼}"

SLEEVE

{17-17¼-17½}
{17¾-18-18¼}"

{14½-14¾-15}
{15¼-15½-15¾}"

2½"

{7½-8-8½}
{9-9-9¼}"

man's v-neck vest

◼◼◼◻ INTERMEDIATE

Size	Finished Chest Measurement	
36	38"	(96.5 cm)
38	40"	(101.5 cm)
40	42½"	(108 cm)
42	44½"	(113 cm)
44	46"	(117 cm)
46	48"	(122 cm)

Size Note: Instructions are written with sizes 36, 38, and 40 in the first set of braces { } and sizes 42, 44, and 46 in the second set of braces. Instructions will be easier to read if you circle all the numbers pertaining to your size. If only one number is given, it applies to all sizes.

This timeless style will add warmth to his wardrobe, as well as good looks. Perfect for weekend get-togethers or casual days at the office.

MATERIALS

Deborah Norville Collection, Serenity Worsted Weight Yarn **MEDIUM 4**
  [3.5 ounces, 186 yards (100 grams, 170 meters) per skein]:
    #44 Lion - {4-5-5}{5-5-6} skeins
Straight knitting needles, sizes 7 (4.5 mm) **and** 9 (5.5 mm) **or** sizes needed for gauge
16" (40.5 cm) Circular knitting needle, size 7 (4.5 mm)
Stitch holder
Markers
Yarn needle

◆**GAUGE:** With larger size needles, in Stockinette Stitch, 18 sts and 23 rows = 4" (10 cm)

Instructions continue on page 26.

Classic. Gorgeous.
Make it as shown for
your man or size it
down for yourself.
—Deborah

BACK
RIBBING
Using smaller size straight needles, cast on {88-92-98} {102-106-110} sts.

Work in K1, P1 ribbing for 2" (5 cm).

BODY
Change to larger size needles.

Work in Stockinette Stitch (knit one row, purl one row) until piece measures approximately 16" (40.5 cm) from cast on edge, ending by working a **purl** row.

ARMHOLE SHAPING
Rows 1 and 2: Bind off {5-5-6}{6-7-8} sts, work across: {78-82-86}{90-92-94} sts.

Row 3 (Decrease row)**:** K1, SSK **(Figs. 9a-c, page 75)**, knit across to last 3 sts, K2 tog **(Fig. 8, page 75)**, K1: {76-80-84} {88-90-92} sts.

Row 4 (Decrease row)**:** P1, P2 tog **(Fig. 11, page 76)**, purl across to last 3 sts, SSP **(Fig. 12, page 76)**, P1: {74-78-82}{86-88-90} sts.

Continue to decrease one stitch at **each** Armhole edge, every row, {2-2-3}{3-3-3} times **more**; then decrease every other row, {3-4-4}{5-5-5} times: {64-66-68}{70-72-74} sts.

Work even until Armholes measure approximately {10-10½-10½}{11-11-11½}"/ {25.5-26.5-26.5}{28-28-29} cm, ending by working a **purl** row.

SHOULDER SHAPING
Rows 1-4: Bind off {6-6-6}{6-6-7} sts, work across: {40-42-44}{46-48-46} sts.

Rows 5 and 6: Bind off {6-6-7}{7-7-6} sts, work across: {28-30-30}{32-34-34} sts.

Slip remaining sts onto st holder; cut yarn.

FRONT
Work same as Back until Armholes measure approximately {4-4½-4¼}{4¾-4½-5}"/ {10-11.5-11}{12-11.5-12.5} cm, ending by working a **purl** row: {64-66-68}{70-72-74} sts.

NECK SHAPING
Both sides of Neck are worked at the same time, using separate yarn for **each** side.

Row 1 (Decrease row)**:** Knit {29-30-31}{32-33-34} sts, K2 tog, K1; with second yarn, K1, SSK, knit across: {31-32-33}{34-35-36} sts **each** side.

Row 2: Purl across; with second yarn, purl across.

Row 3 (Decrease row)**:** Knit across to within 3 sts of Neck edge, K2 tog, K1; with second yarn, K1, SSK, knit across: {30-31-32}{33-34-35} sts **each** side.

Repeat Rows 2 and 3, {12-13-13}{14-15-15} times: {18-18-19}{19-19-20} sts **each** side.

Work even until Armholes measure same as Back, ending by working a **purl** row.

SHOULDER SHAPING
Rows 1-4: Bind off {6-6-6}{6-6-7} sts at Armhole edge, work across; with second yarn, work across: {6-6-7}{7-7-6} sts **each** side.

Row 5: Bind off remaining sts on first side leaving a long end for sewing; with second yarn, knit across.

Bind off remaining sts leaving a long end for sewing.

FINISHING

Using long ends, sew shoulder seams.

NECK RIBBING

With **right** side facing and using circular needle, pick up {30-30-32}{32-34-34} sts evenly spaced along left Front Neck edge *(Fig. 17a, page 79)*, place marker *(see Markers, page 70)*, pick up {29-29-31}{31-33-33} sts evenly spaced along right Front Neck edge, slip {28-30-30}{32-34-34} sts from Back st holder onto second end of circular needle and knit across, place marker to mark beginning of rnd: {87-89-93}{95-101-101} sts.

Rnd 1 (Decrease rnd)**:** (K1, P1) across to within 2 sts of next marker, K2 tog, SSK, P1, (K1, P1) around: {85-87-91}{93-99-99} sts.

Rnds 2 and 3 (Decrease rnds)**:** Work in established ribbing across to within 2 sts of next marker, K2 tog, SSK, work in established ribbing around: {81-83-87}{89-95-95} sts.

Bind off all sts in ribbing.

ARMHOLE RIBBING

With **right** side facing and using smaller size straight needle, pick up {90-94-94}{100-100-104} sts evenly spaced along Armhole edge.

Work in K1, P1 ribbing for 3 rows.

Bind off all sts in ribbing.

Repeat for second Armhole.

Weave side seams *(Fig. 15, page 78)*.

Note: Vest width includes 2 edge stitches.

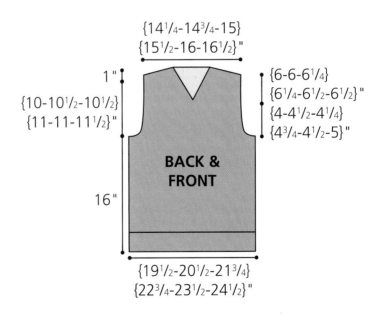

{14¼-14¾-15}
{15½-16-16½}"

1"

{10-10½-10½}
{11-11-11½}"

{6-6-6¼}
{6¼-6½-6½}"
{4-4½-4¼}
{4¾-4½-5}"

BACK & FRONT

16"

{19½-20½-21¾}
{22¾-23½-24½}"

lace scarf & shawl

■■□□ EASY

Finished Sizes

Scarf: unblocked 5³/₄" x 65" (14.5 cm x 165 cm)
blocked 7¹/₂" x 84" (19 cm x 213 cm)
Shawl: unblocked 15³/₄" x 65" (40 cm x 165 cm)
blocked 20¹/₂" x 84" (52 cm x 213 cm)

When just a wisp of warmth is enough, these lacy accessories will do the job with a soft, feminine touch—they also prove the versatility of Serenity Sock Weight Yarn! The scarf pattern includes the variation to create the shawl.

MATERIALS

Deborah Norville Collection, Serenity Sock Weight Yarn
[1.76 ounces, 230 yards (50 grams, 210 meters) per skein]:
Scarf #04-01 Tyme - 2 skeins
Shawl #04-07 Chili - 4 skeins
Straight knitting needles, size 8 (5 mm) **or** size needed for gauge
Pins for Blocking

◆GAUGE: In Stockinette Stitch, 20 sts and 28 rows = 4" (10 cm)

When blocked, Scarf and Shawl will stretch approximately 20% to 30%.

Instructions are written for Scarf with numbers for Shawl in braces { }. Circle all the numbers pertaining to the one you are making.

Instructions continue on page 30.

EYELET EDGE

Cast on 33{93} sts **loosely**.

Row 1: Knit across.

Row 2 (Right side): Slip 1 as if to **knit**, K1, K2 tog **(Fig. 8, page 75)**, YO **(Fig. 3a, page 73)**, K1, ★ YO, [slip 1 as if to **knit**, K2 tog, PSSO **(Figs. 10a & b, page 76)**], K2 tog, YO, K1; repeat from ★ across to last 4 sts, YO, SSK **(Figs. 9a-c, page 75)**, K2: 29{79} sts.

Row 3: Slip 1 as if to **knit**, K1, purl across to last 2 sts, K2.

Row 4: Slip 1 as if to **knit**, K1, ★ K2 tog, YO, K1, YO, SSK; repeat from ★ across to last 2 sts, K2.

Rows 5-41: Repeat Rows 3 and 4, 18 times; then repeat Row 3 once **more**.

BODY

Row 1: Slip 1 as if to **knit**, K1, K2 tog, YO, K1, YO, SSK, ★ K5, K2 tog, YO, K1, YO, SSK; repeat from ★ across to last 2 sts, K2.

Row 2: Slip 1 as if to **knit**, K1, purl across to last 2 sts, K2.

Repeat Rows 1 and 2 for pattern until piece measures approximately 58" (147.5 cm) from cast on edge **or** to desired length, ending by working Row 2.

EYELET EDGE

Row 1: Slip 1 as if to **knit**, K1, ★ K2 tog, YO, K1, YO, SSK; repea from ★ across to last 2 sts, K2.

Row 2: Slip 1 as if to **knit**, K1, purl across to last 2 sts, K2.

Rows 3-40: Repeat Rows 1 and 2, 19 times.

Row 41: Slip 1 as if to **knit**, K1, K2 tog, YO, K1, YO, SSK, ★ YO, K2 tog, YO, K1, YO, SSK; repeat from ★ across to last 2 sts, K2: 33{93} sts.

Row 42: Slip 1 as if to **knit**, knit across.

Bind off all sts **very loosely** in **knit**.

CARE AND BLOCKING

Gently hand wash your project in mild soap. Rinse it gently, if necessary. Place your project in the washer set on spin cycle to remove excess water. Lay out wet project to blocked dimension and pin it in place. Let it dry overnight.

Designs by Kay Meadors.

This shawl dresses up this solid dress with its variegated pattern— wouldn't a solid black be super elegant for evenings out?

— Deborah

I am a fiend for mittens. Solids, stripes…what about using your favorite colors and "inventing" your own stripe pattern?

—Deborah

These mittens are excellent gifts for everyone in the family. Sizes are for children through adults. Leave them solid or change colors to create them in stripes. Have fun making no two pairs alike!

Instructions begin on page 32.

Size	Hand Circumference
Child	
Small	5¹/₂" (14 cm)
Medium	6" (15 cm)
Large	6³/₄" (17 cm)
Adult	
Small	7¹/₄" (18.5 cm)
Medium	8" (20.5 cm)
Large	8¹/₂" (21.5 cm)

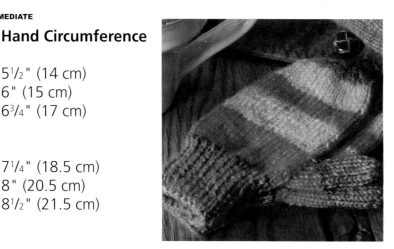

Size Note: Instructions are written with Child sizes in the first set of braces { } and Adult sizes in the second set of braces. Instructions will be easier to read if you circle all the numbers pertaining to your size. If only one number is given, it applies to all sizes.

MATERIALS
Deborah Norville Collection, Serenity Sport Weight Yarn 🄶2
[3.5 ounces, 361 yards (100 grams, 330 meters) per skein]:
Solid
#29 Marina Blue - 1 skein
Stripes
Color A #18 Rosebud - 1 skein
Color B #24 Pool Blue - 1 skein
Color C #29 Marina Blue - 1 skein
Set of 4 double pointed knitting needles, sizes 2 (2.75 mm)
and 3 (3.25 mm) **or** sizes needed for gauge
Stitch holder
Split-ring markers
Tapestry needle

♦**GAUGE:** With larger size needles, in Stockinette Stitch,
13 sts and 16 rows = 2" (5 cm)

The Adult size was made with one color and the Child's size was made with three colors. Stripe your mittens as desired.

RIGHT MITTEN
CUFF
Using smaller size needles, cast on {36-40-44}{48-52-56} sts and divide evenly on 3 needles **(see Using Double Pointed Needles, page 72)**.

Place a split-ring marker around the first stitch to indicate the beginning of the round **(see Markers, page 70)**.

Work in K1, P1 ribbing for {1¹/₂-2-2¹/₂}{3-3-3}"/{4-5-6.5}{7.5-7.5-7.5} cm.

HAND
Change to larger size needles.

Knit {2-3-4}{4-5-6} rounds.

THUMB GUSSET
Rnd 1 (Increase rnd)**:** K2, work right invisible increase **(Fig. 6, page 74)**, K1, work left invisible increase **(Figs. 7a & b, page 75)**, place marker, knit around: {38-42-46}{50-54-58} sts.

Rnd 2: Knit around.

Rnd 3 (Increase rnd)**:** K2, work right invisible increase, knit across to next marker, work left invisible increase, slip marker, knit around: {40-44-48}{52-56-60} sts.

Rnd 4: Knit around.

Repeat Rnds 3 and 4, {2-3-5}{6-7-8} times: {44-50-58}{64-70-76} sts.

Dividing Rnd: K2, slip next {9-11-15}{17-19-21} sts onto st holder, remove marker, work left invisible increase, knit around: {36-40-44}{48-52-56} sts.

Work even until Mitten measures approximately {5-6½-7} {9-9½-10}"/{12.5-16.5-18} {23-24-25.5} cm from cast on edge **or** to desired length.

TOP SHAPING
Rnd 1 (Decrease rnd)**:** (K2, K2 tog) around **(Fig. 8, page 75)**: {27-30-33} {36-39-42} sts.

Rnds 2 and 3: Knit around.

Rnd 4 (Decrease rnd)**:** (K1, K2 tog) around: {18-20-22} {24-26-28} sts.

Rnds 5 and 6: Knit around.

Rnd 7 (Decrease rnd)**:** K2 tog around: {9-10-11}{12-13-14} sts.

Cut yarn leaving a long end for sewing. Thread tapestry needle with end and slip remaining sts onto tapestry needle; gather tightly to close and secure end.

THUMB
Rnd 1: Divide sts from st holder evenly on 3 needles; make one **(Figs. 5a & b, page 74)**, knit around: {10-12-16}{18-20-22} sts.

Work even until Thumb measures approximately {1-1½-2} {2¼-2½-2¾}"/{2.5-4-5} {5.5-6.5-7} cm **or** to desired length.

Decrease Rnd: K2 tog around: {5-6-8}{9-10-11} sts.

Cut yarn leaving a long end for sewing. Thread tapestry needle with yarn end and slip remaining sts onto tapestry needle; gather tightly to close and secure end.

LEFT MITTEN
Work same as Right Mitten to Thumb Gusset.

THUMB GUSSET
Rnd 1 (Increase rnd)**:** Knit {33-37-41}{45-49-53} sts, place marker, work right invisible increase, K1, work left invisible increase, K2: {38-42-46} {50-54-58} sts.

Rnd 2: Knit around.

Rnd 3 (Increase rnd)**:** Knit across to next marker, slip marker, work right invisible increase, knit across to within 2 sts of marker, work left invisible increase, K2: {40-44-48}{52-56-60} sts.

Rnd 4: Knit around.

Repeat Rnds 3 and 4, {2-3-5}{6-7-8} times: {44-50-58}{64-70-76} sts.

Dividing Rnd: Knit across to marker, remove marker, slip next {9-11-15}{17-19-21} sts onto st holder, work left invisible increase, K2: {36-40-44} {48-52-56} sts.

Work even until Mitten measures approximately {5-6½-7} {9-9½-10}"/{12.5-16.5-18} {23-24-25.5} cm from cast on edge **or** to desired length.

Complete same as Right Mitten, beginning with Top Shaping.

Design by Marion Graham.

Finished Size:
7¼" (18.5 cm) around hand by 6" (15 cm) long

MATERIALS
Deborah Norville Collection, Serenity Chunky Weight Yarn 🄵**5** BULKY
[3.5 ounces, 109 yards (100 grams, 100 meters) per skein]:
 #04 Pink Candy - 1 skein
Straight knitting needles, size 11 (8 mm) **or** size needed for gauge
Yarn needle

♦**GAUGE:** In Stockinette Stitch, 12 sts and 15 rows = 4" (10 cm)

Knitting doesn't get easier than this! For each hand mitt, you use Serenity Chunky Weight Yarn to knit a rectangle; then sew two opposing edges together, leaving a hole for your thumb. Now you can keep your fingers free to operate MP3 players or other handheld devices.

WRIST RIBBING
Leaving a long end for sewing, cast on 24 sts.

Row 1: (K1, P1) across.

Repeat Row 1 until Wrist Ribbing measures 2" (5 cm).

BODY
Work in Stockinette Stitch (knit one row, purl one row) until piece measures approximately 4" (10 cm) from cast on edge.

TOP RIBBING
Row 1: (K1, P1) across.

Repeat Row 1 until Top Ribbing measures 2" (5 cm).

Bind off all sts in ribbing, leaving a long end for sewing.

FINISHING
Thread the yarn needle with the first long end. Fold the Hand Mitt with the **right** side facing you and the edges lined up. Weave the Wrist Ribbing and the Body for the first 2½" (6.5 cm) **(Fig. 15, page 78)**.

Thread yarn needle with second yarn end. Weave the Top Ribbing and the Body for 2¼" (5.5 cm), leaving a 1¼" (3 cm) opening for your thumb.

Repeat for second Hand Mitt.

ribbed hat

Size	Head Circumference		Finished Measurement	
Child				
Small	16½"	(42 cm)	14½"	(37 cm)
Medium	18"	(45.5 cm)	16"	(40.5 cm)
Large	19½"	(49.5 cm)	17½"	(44.5 cm)
Adult				
Small	21"	(53.5 cm)	19"	(48.5 cm)
Medium	22½"	(57 cm)	20½"	(52 cm)
Large	24"	(61 cm)	22"	(56 cm)

There's a toasty hat in this flexible pattern for everyone, children through adults! The deeply ribbed design can be knitted using one strand of Serenity Chunky Weight Yarn. Or you can create a tweed look by holding two strands of complementary Serenity Worsted Weight Yarns together.

Size Note: Instructions are written with Child sizes in the first set of braces { } and Adult sizes in the second set of braces. Instructions will be easier to read if you circle all the numbers pertaining to your size. If only one number is given, it applies to all sizes.

MATERIALS

Deborah Norville Collection, Serenity Chunky Weight Yarn **BULKY 5**
[3.5 ounces, 109 yards (100 grams, 100 meters) per skein]:
option 1: #07 Seven Seas **or** option 2: #10 Apple Orchard - {1-1-2}{2-2-2} skein(s) **each** option

or

Worsted Weight Yarn **MEDIUM 4**
[3.5 ounces, 186 yards (100 grams, 170 meters) per skein]:
option 3: #32 True Blue - {1-1-1}{1-2-2} skein(s)
option 4: #33 Kiwi and #34 Green - 1 skein **each**
option 5: #32 True Blue, #33 Kiwi, and #34 Green - 1 skein **each**
Straight knitting needles, size 9 (5.5 mm) **or** size needed for gauge
Markers
Yarn needle

The Hats can be made with one strand of Bulky Weight Yarn or by holding two strands of Worsted Weight Yarn together.

♦**GAUGE:** In Ribbing, 8 sts and 10 rows = 2" (5 cm)

This picture makes me want to knit up toboggan hats for every member of my family (and then make them wear them when we take our Christmas card photo!). You can use the same yarns, but make each hat unique just by mixing up the yarns!

— Deborah

BODY

Stripe your hat as desired.

Cast on {60-66-72}{78-84-90} sts **loosely**.

Work in K1, P1 ribbing for {7-8-9}{10-11-12}"/{18-20.5-23} {25.5-28-30.5} cm.

TOP SHAPING

Row 1 (Decrease row)**:** Knit {8-9-10}{11-12-13} sts, K2 tog **(Fig. 8, page 75)**, ★ place marker **(see Markers, page 70)**, knit {8-9-10}{11-12-13} sts, K2 tog; repeat from ★ across: {54-60-66}{72-78-84} sts.

Row 2: Purl across.

Row 3 (Decrease row)**:** ★ Knit across to within 2 sts of next marker, K2 tog; repeat from ★ 4 times **more**, knit across to last 2 sts, K2 tog: {48-54-60} {66-72-78} sts.

Repeat Rows 2 and 3, {6-7-8}{9-10-11} times: 12 sts.

Cut yarn leaving a long end for sewing.

Thread yarn needle with end and slip remaining sts onto yarn needle; gather tightly to close and secure end. Weave seam reversing seam halfway through Body so seam won't show when cuff is turned up **(Fig. 15, page 78)**.

Add pom-pom if desired **(Figs. 18a-c, page 80)**.

Design by Marion Graham.

◐■☐☐ **EASY**

Finished Size: Adult
Head Circumferece: 20" (51 cm)

MATERIALS

Deborah Norville Collection, Serenity Worsted Weight Yarn

[3.5 ounces, 186 yards (100 grams, 170 meters) per skein]:
  Main Color #50 Steel - 1 skein
  Color A #29 Marina Blue - 1 skein
  Color B #34 Green - 1 skein
Straight knitting needles, size 8 (5 mm) **or** size needed for gauge
Yarn needle

◆**GAUGE:** In pattern, 15 sts and 20 rows = 3" (7.5 cm)

Knit with just a single strand of Serenity Worsted Weight Yarn, this striped hat is light and comfortable. The pattern is easy, too.

RIBBING

With Main Color, cast on 92 sts.

Row 1: P1, K1, (P2, K1) across to last 3 sts, P3.

Row 2 (Right side)**:** K3, P1, (K2, P1) across to last st, K1.

Rows 3-8: Repeat Rows 1 and 2, 3 times.

BODY

Row 1: P1, knit across to last st, P1.

Row 2: K3, P1, (K2, P1) across to last st, K1.

Row 3: P1, K1, (P2, K1) across to last 3 sts, P3.

Row 4: K3, P1, (K2, P1) across to last st, K1.

Row 5: P1, knit across to last st, P1.

Carry unused Main Color along side of piece, twisting yarns every other row.

Rows 6-9: Drop Main Color; with Color A repeat Rows 2-5.

Rows 10-17: Cut Color A; with Main Color repeat Rows 2-5 twice.

Rows 18-21: Drop Main Color; with Color B repeat Rows 2-5.

Rows 22-29: Cut Color B; with Main Color repeat Rows 2-5 twice.

Rows 30-33: Drop Main Color; with Color A repeat Rows 2-5.

TOP SHAPING

Row 1: Cut Color A, with Main Color K1, ★ K2 tog *(Fig. 8, page 75)*, P1, (K2, P1) twice; repeat from ★ across to last st, K1: 82 sts.

Row 2: ★ P1, K1, (P2, K1) twice; repeat from ★ across to last 2 sts, P2.

Row 3: K2, ★ P1, K2 tog, P1, K2, P1, K1; repeat from ★ across: 72 sts.

Row 4: P1, knit across to last st, P1.

Row 5: K2, P1, K1, P1, K2 tog, P1, ★ (K1, P1) twice, K2 tog, P1; repeat from ★ across to last st, K1: 62 sts.

Row 6: (P1, K1) across to last 2 sts, P2.

Row 7: K1, SSK across to last st *(Figs. 9a-c, page 75)*, K1: 32 sts.

Row 8: P1, knit across to last st, P1.

Row 9: K1, K2 tog across to last st, K1: 17 sts.

This hat is beyond easy—and every time you make it, it can be different. Try it with a bright main color and then do the contrast stripes in various intensities of the same hue.

—Deborah

Row 10: P1, P2 tog across to last 2 sts *(Fig. 11, page 76)*, P2: 10 sts.

Cut yarn leaving a long end for sewing.

Thread yarn needle with yarn end and slip remaining sts onto yarn needle; gather tightly to close and secure end; weave seam *(Fig. 15, page 78)*.

Design by Lois J. Long.

neck warmer

Finished Size: 6" x 25" (15 cm x 63.5 cm)

MATERIALS

Deborah Norville Collection, Serenity Chunky Weight Yarn **⑤** **BULKY**
[3.5 ounces, 109 yards (100 grams, 100 meters) per skein]:
#05 Citrus - 1 skein
Straight knitting needles, size 11 (8 mm) **or** size needed for gauge

♦**GAUGE:** In Seed Stitch, 12 sts and 22 rows = 4" (10 cm)

BODY

Cast on 19 sts.

Rows 1-5: K1, (P1, K1) across.

Tip: It takes two stitches to bind off the first stitch.

Row 6: K1, (P1, K1) twice, bind off next 9 sts in pattern (opening), (P1, K1) twice: 5 sts **each** side.

Row 7: K1, (P1, K1) twice; **turn**, add on 9 sts *(Figs. 2a & b, page 72)*; **turn**, K1, (P1, K1) twice: 19 sts.

Repeat Row 1 for Seed Stitch until Body measures approximately 25" (63.5 cm) from cast on edge.

Bind off all sts in pattern.

A great design for beginning knitters, this fashionable neck warmer uses Serenity Chunky Weight Yarn–which also makes it a quick gift. To wear, just pull one end of the warmer through the opening in the other end.

The seed stitch of this pattern really brings out the variegation of the Serenity Chunky Weight Yarn—which is so soft, you won't believe it's not expensive cashmere.

—Deborah

baby blanket

◖◼◻◻ **EASY +**

Finished Size: 40" (101.5 cm) square

MATERIALS

Deborah Norville Collection, Serenity Worsted Weight Yarn
[3.5 ounces, 186 yards (100 grams, 170 meters) per skein]:
#23 Aqua - 7 skeins
31" (78.5 cm) Circular knitting needle, size 9 (5.5 mm) **or**
size needed for gauge

◆**GAUGE:** In Diagonal Moss Stitch,18 sts and 23 rows = 4" (10 cm)

Gauge Swatch: 4¹/₂" x 4" (11.5 cm x 10 cm)
Cast on 20 sts.
Rows 1 and 2: (K2, P2) across.
Row 3: K1, P2, (K2, P2) across to last st, K1.
Row 4: P1, K2, (P2, K2) across to last st, P1.
Rows 5 and 6: (P2, K2) across.
Row 7: P1, K2, (P2, K2) across to last st, P1.
Row 8: K1, P2, (K2, P2) across to last st, K1.
Rows 9-23: Repeat Rows 1-8 once for Diagonal Moss St, then repeat
Rows 1-7 once **more**.
Bind off all sts in pattern.

Diagonal Moss Stitch creates a pattern running obliquely across the center of this baby blanket, while the border adds intriguing texture. The lovely design uses Serenity Worsted Weight Yarn, and it's sure to become your favorite gift to make for baby showers.

*This pattern only **looks** hard. You'll be amazed how fast you master the diagonal moss stitch.*

—Deborah

BOTTOM BORDER

Cast on 180 sts.

Rows 1 and 2: (K2, P2) across.

Rows 3 and 4: (P2, K2) across.

Rows 5-12: Repeat Rows 1-4 twice.

Rows 13 and 14: (K2, P2) twice, knit across to last 6 sts, P2, K2, P2.

Rows 15 and 16: P2, K2, P2, knit across to last 8 sts, (P2, K2) twice.

Rows 17 and 18: (K2, P2) twice, knit across to last 6 sts, P2, K2, P2.

BODY

Rows 1 and 2: P2, K2, P2, K8, P2, (K2, P2) across to last 12 sts, K4, (P2, K2) twice.

Row 3: (K2, P2) twice, K5, P2, (K2, P2) across to last 13 sts, K7, P2, K2, P2.

Row 4: (K2, P2) twice, K4, P1, K2, (P2, K2) across to last 13 sts, P1, K6, P2, K2, P2.

Rows 5 and 6: P2, K2, P2, K6, P2, (K2, P2) across to last 14 sts, K6, (P2, K2) twice.

Row 7: (K2, P2) twice, K4, P1, K2, (P2, K2) across to last 13 sts, P1, K6, P2, K2, P2.

Row 8: (K2, P2) twice, K5, P2, (K2, P2) across to last 13 sts, K7, P2, K2, P2.

Repeat Rows 1-8 for pattern until Blanket measures approximately 36³/₄" (93.5 cm) from cast on edge, ending by working Row 6.

TOP BORDER

Rows 1-6: Repeat Rows 13-18 of Bottom Border.

Rows 7 and 8: (P2, K2) across.

Rows 9 and 10: (K2, P2) across.

Rows 11-18: Repeat Rows 7-10 twice.

Bind off all sts in pattern.

43

Cute. Quick.

What else is there to say?

—Deborah

The soft ribbing on these little booties will keep them on Baby's feet without the use of fasteners. Because Serenity Sport Weight Yarn and Worsted Weight Yarn share the same color palette, the booties match the blanket on page 43 and the jacket on page 47.

baby booties

◖◼◻◻ **EASY +**

Finished Size: Newborn and 6 months

Size Note: Instructions are written for newborn with size 6 months in braces { }. Instructions will be easier to read if you circle all the numbers pertaining to your baby's size. If only one number is given, it applies to both sizes.

MATERIALS
Deborah Norville Collection, Serenity Sport Weight Yarn **2**
   [3.5 ounces, 361 yards (100 grams, 330 meters) per skein]:
      #23 Aqua - 1 skein
Straight knitting needles, sizes 2 (2.75 mm) **and**
   3 (3.25 mm) **or** sizes needed for gauge
Stitch holders - 2
Tapestry needle

GAUGE: With larger size needles, in Double Moss St, 3 sts and 18 rows = 2" (5 cm)

Gauge Swatch: 2½" x 2" (5.25 cm x 5 cm)
Cast on 16 sts.
Rows 1 and 2: (K2, P2) across.
Rows 3 and 4: (P2, K2) across.
Rows 5-18: Repeat Rows 1-4, times; then repeat Rows 1 and once **more**.
Bind off all sts in pattern.

CUFF

With smaller size needles and leaving a long end for sewing, cast on 34{38} sts.

Row 1: P2, (K2, P2) across.

Row 2 (Right side)**:** K2, (P2, K2) across.

Repeat Rows 1 and 2 until Cuff measures approximately ½{2}"/4{5} cm from cast on edge, ending by working Row 1.

INSTEP

Change to larger size needles.

SIZE NEWBORN ONLY
Row 1: Work across 12 sts in established ribbing, slip sts just worked onto st holder, K3, P2, K2, P3, slip remaining 12 sts onto second st holder: 10 sts.

Row 2: K3, P2, K2, P3.

Rows 3 and 4: P3, K2, P2, K3.

Rows 5 and 6: K3, P2, K2, P3.

Rows 7-12: Repeat Rows 3-6 once; then repeat Rows 3 and 4 once **more**.

SIZE 6 MONTHS ONLY
Row 1: Work across 13 sts in established ribbing, slip sts just worked onto st holder, K3, P2, K2, P2, K3, slip remaining 13 sts onto second st holder: 12 sts.

Rows 2 and 3: P3, K2, P2, K2, P3.

Rows 4 and 5: K3, P2, K2, P2, K3.

Rows 6-16: Repeat Rows 2-5 twice; then repeat Rows 2-4 once **more**.

BOTH SIZES
Row 13{17} (Decrease row)**:** Decrease **(see Decreases, pages 75 and 76)**, work across in pattern to last 2 sts, decrease: 8{10} sts.

Row 14{18}: Work across in pattern.

Repeat last 2 rows: 6{8} sts.

Cut yarn.

SIDES
Row 1: With **right** side facing, knit sts from first st holder, pick up 10{14} sts evenly spaced along Instep **(Fig. 17a, page 79)**, K 6{8}, pick up 10{14} sts evenly spaced along second side of Instep, slip sts from st holder onto empty needle and knit across: 50{62} sts.

Row 2: Knit across.

Row 3: K2, (P2, K2) across.

Rows 4 and 5: P2, (K2, P2) across.

Rows 6 and 7: K2, (P2, K2) across.

Row 8: P2, (K2, P2) across.

SIZE 6 MONTHS ONLY
Rows 9 and 10: Repeat Rows 5 and 6.

SOLE
Row 1: K2 tog, K 21{27}, K2 tog twice, K 21{27}, K2 tog: 46{58} sts.

Row 2: Purl across.

Row 3: K2 tog, K 19{25}, K2 tog twice, K 19{25}, K2 tog: 42{54} sts.

SIZE 6 MONTHS ONLY
Row 4: Purl across.

Row 5: K2 tog, K 23, K2 tog twice, K 23, K2 tog: 50 sts.

BOTH SIZES
Bind off all sts in **purl**.

Weave Back seam **(Fig. 15, page 78)**. Join bound off sts to form Sole seam **(Figs. 16a & b, page 78)**.

baby jacket

◼◼◼▢ **INTERMEDIATE +**

Size	Finished Chest Measurement
3 months	17¼" (44 cm)
6 months	18½" (47 cm)
12 months	19½" (49.5 cm)
18 months	21" (53.5 cm)

Size Note: Instructions are written for size 3 months with sizes 6, 12 and 18 months in braces { }. Instructions will be easier to read if you circle all the numbers pertaining to your baby's size. If only one number is given, it applies to all sizes.

MATERIALS

Deborah Norville Collection, Serenity Sport Weight Yarn 🄂
[3.5 ounces, 361 yards (100 grams, 330 meters) per skein]:
    #23 Aqua - 1{2-2-2} skein(s)
Straight knitting needles, sizes 2 (2.75 mm) **and** 3 (3.25 mm) **or** sizes needed for gauge
Split-ring markers
Stitch holders - 3
Separating zipper - 10" (25.5 cm)
½" (12 mm) Buttons - 2
Sewing needle and thread
Tapestry needle

GAUGE: With larger size needles, in Double Moss Stitch, 26 sts and 36 rows = 4" (10 cm)

Gauge Swatch: 4" (10 cm) square
Cast on 26 sts.
Work same as Back Body, page 48, for 36 rows.
Bind off all sts in pattern.

Pure sweetness! That precious little one will be picture-perfect in this zip-up jacket.

Instructions continue on page 48

My grandmother made baby sweaters constantly, even when no one in the family was expecting! With this pattern, you may find that you, too, make oodles of sweaters. And don't be afraid to experiment with colors—wouldn't contrast ribbing look cute?

—Deborah

BACK
RIBBING
Using smaller size needles, cast on 58{62-66-70} sts.

Row 1: P2, (K2, P2) across.

Row 2 (Right side)**:** K2, (P2, K2) across.

Note: Loop a short piece of yarn around any stitch to mark Row 2 as **right** side.

Rows 3-15: Repeat Rows 1 and 2, 6 times; then repeat Row 1 once **more**.

BODY
Change to larger size needles.

Row 1: P2, (K2, P2) across.

Rows 2 and 3: K2, (P2, K2) across.

Rows 4 and 5: P2, (K2, P2) across.

Repeat Rows 2-5 for Double Moss Stitch until Back measures approximately 6^3/$_4${7^1/$_2$-8^1/$_4$-8^1/$_2$}"/ 17{19-21-21.5} cm from cast on edge, ending by working Row 3 or 5.

YOKE
Rows 1-5: Knit across.

Double Moss Stitch will be worked on center 8{12-16-12} sts with Diagonal Moss Stitch worked on each side.

Row 6: P3, K2, (P2, K2) 5{5-5-6} times, P1, K2, (P2, K2) 1{2-3-2} time(s), P1, K2, (P2, K2) across to last 3 sts, P3.

Row 7: K3, P2, (K2, P2) 5{5-5-6} times, K1, P2, (K2, P2) 1{2-3-2} time(s), K1, P2, (K2, P2) across to last 3 sts, K3.

Row 8: (P2, K2) 6{6-6-7} times, P4, K2, (P2, K2) 0{1-2-1} time(s) *(see Zeros, page 71)*, P4, (K2, P2) across.

Row 9: (K2, P2) 6{6-6-7} times, K4, P2, (K2, P2) 0{1-2-1} time(s), K4, (P2, K2) across.

Row 10: K3, (P2, K2) 5{5-5-6} times, P3, K2, (P2, K2) 1{2-3-2} time(s), P3, (K2, P2) across to last 3 sts, K3.

Row 11: P3, (K2, P2) 5{5-5-6} times, K3, P2, (K2, P2) 1{2-3-2} time(s), K3, (P2, K2) across to last 3 sts, P3.

Row 12: (K2, P2) 6{6-6-7} times, K1, P3, K2, (P2, K2) 0{1-2-1} time(s), P3, K1, (P2, K2) across.

Row 13: (P2, K2) 6{6-6-7} times, P1, K3, P2, (K2, P2) 0{1-2-1} time(s), K3, P1, (K2, P2) across.

Repeat Rows 6-13 for pattern until Back measures approximately 9^1/$_2${10^1/$_2$-11^1/$_2$-12}"/ 24{26.5-29-30.5} cm from cast on edge, ending by working a **wrong** side row.

NECK SHAPING
Both sides of Neck are worked at the same time, using separate yarn for **each** side. Maintain established pattern throughout.

Row 1: Work across 22{23-25-27} sts, slip next 14{16-16-16} sts onto st holder; with second yarn, work across: 22{23-25-27} sts **each** side.

Rows 2-4: Work across to within 2 sts of Neck edge, decrease *(see Decreases, pages 75 and 76)*; with second yarn, decrease, work across: 19{20-22-24} sts **each** side.

Bind off all sts in pattern.

LEFT FRONT
RIBBING
Using smaller size needles, cast on 28{30-32-34} sts.

Row 1: P 0{2-0-2}, (K2, P2) across.

Row 2 (Right side)**:** (K2, P2) across to last 0{2-0-2} sts, K 0{2-0-2}.

Note: Mark Row 2 as **right** side.

Rows 3-15: Repeat Rows 1 and 2, 6 times; then repeat Row 1 once **more**.

BODY

Change to larger size needles.

Row 1: (P2, K2) across to last 0{2-0-2} sts, P 0{2-0-2}.

Row 2: K 0{2-0-2}, (P2, K2) across.

Row 3: (K2, P2) across to last 0{2-0-2} sts, K 0{2-0-2}.

Row 4: P 0{2-0-2}, (K2, P2) across.

Repeat Rows 1-4 for Double Moss Stitch until Left Front measures same as Back to Yoke, ending by working Row 1 or 3.

YOKE

Rows 1-5: Knit across.

Row 6: (K2, P2) across to last 0{2-0-2} sts, K 0{2-0-2}.

Row 7: P 0{2-0-2}, (K2, P2) across.

Row 8: P3, K2, (P2, K2) across to last 3{5-3-5} sts, P3{2-3-2}, K 0{3-0-3}.

Row 9: P 0{3-0-3}, K3{2-3-2}, P2, (K2, P2) across to last 3 sts, K3.

Row 10: (P2, K2) across to last 0{2-0-2} sts, P 0{2-0-2}.

Row 11: K 0{2-0-2}, (P2, K2) across.

Row 12: K3, (P2, K2) across to last 5{3-5-3} sts, P2{3-2-3}, K3{0-3-0}.

Row 13: P3{0-3-0}, K2{3-2-3}, (P2, K2) across to last 3 sts, P3.

NECK SHAPING

Maintain established pattern throughout.

Row 1: Work across to last 4{5-5-5} sts, slip remaining sts onto st holder: 24{25-27-29} sts.

Row 2 (Decrease row): Decrease, work across: 23{24-26-28} sts.

Row 3 (Decrease row): Work across to last 2 sts, decrease: 22{23-25-27} sts.

Row 4 (Decrease row): Decrease, work across: 21{22-24-26} sts.

Row 5: Work across.

Rows 6-8: Repeat Rows 4 and 5 once, then repeat Row 4 once **more**: 19{20-22-24} sts.

Work even until Left Front measures same as Back, ending by working a **wrong** side row.

Bind off all sts in pattern leaving a long end for sewing.

RIGHT FRONT
RIBBING

The extra 8 sts on Ribbing form the Buttonhole tab.

Using smaller size needles, cast on 36{38-40-42} sts.

Row 1: (P2, K2) across to last 0{2-0-2} sts, P 0{2-0-2}.

Row 2 (Right side): K 0{2-0-2}, (P2, K2) across.

Note: Mark Row 2 as **right** side.

Row 3: (P2, K2) across to last 0{2-0-2} sts, P 0{2-0-2}.

Tip: It takes two stitches to bind off the first stitch.

Row 4 (Buttonhole row): Maintaining pattern, work 3 sts, bind off next 3 sts (leaving 3 sts on right side of buttonhole), work across: 33{35-37-39} sts.

Row 5: Work across to bound off sts, **turn**; add on 3 sts **(Figs. 2a & b, page 72)**, turn; work across: 36{38-40-42} sts.

Rows 6-9: Repeat Rows 2 and 3 twice.

Rows 10-15: Repeat Rows 4-9.

Instructions continue on page 50.

BODY

Change to larger size needles.

Row 1: Bind off 8 sts for buttonhole tab, P 0{1-0-1}, K1{2-1-2}, P2, (K2, P2) across: 28{30-32-34} sts.

Row 2: (K2, P2) across to last 0{2-0-2} sts, K 0{2-0-2}.

Row 3: K 0{2-0-2}, (P2, K2) across.

Row 4: (P2, K2) across to last 0{2-0-2} sts, P 0{2-0-2}.

Row 5: P 0{2-0-2}, (K2, P2) across.

Repeat Rows 2-5 for Double Moss Stitch until Right Front measures same as Back to Yoke, ending by working Row 3 or 5.

YOKE

Rows 1-5: Knit across.

Row 6: K 0{2-0-2}, (P2, K2) across.

Row 7: (P2, K2) across to last 0{2-0-2} sts, P 0{2-0-2}.

Row 8: K 0{3-0-3}, P3{2-3-2}, K2, (P2, K2) across to last 3 sts, P3.

Row 9: K3, P2, (K2, P2) across to last 3{5-3-5} sts, K3{2-3-2}, P 0{3-0-3}.

Row 10: P 0{2-0-2}, (K2, P2) across.

Row 11: (K2, P2) across to last 0{2-0-2} sts, K 0{2-0-2}.

Row 12: K 3{0-3-0}, P2{3-2-3}, (K2, P2) across to last 3 sts, K3.

Row 13: P3, (K2, P2) across to last 5{3-5-3} sts, K2{3-2-3}, P 3{0-3-0}.

Row 14: K 0{2-0-2}, (P2, K2) across.

NECK SHAPING

Complete same as Left Front.

Using long ends, sew shoulder seams.

Place a split-ring marker on **each** side of Front and Back, 4{4¼-4½-4¾}"/ 10{11-11.5-12} cm down from shoulder seam.

SLEEVE
BODY

With **right** side facing and using larger size needles, pick up 50{54-58-62} sts evenly spaced between markers **(Fig. 17a, page 79)**.

Row 1: P2, (K2, P2) across.

Rows 2 and 3: K2, (P2, K2) across.

A button-tab closure provides a professional finish to Baby's jacket.

Rows 4 and 5: P2, (K2, P2) across.

Rows 6-9: Repeat Rows 2-5.

Work in established Double Moss stitch, decreasing one stitch at each edge, every fourth row, 7{9-12-13} times; then decrease every other row, 2{2-0-1} time(s): 32{32-34-34} sts.

RIBBING

Change to smaller size needles.

Work in K2, P2 ribbing until Sleeve measures approximately 6{7-8-9}"/15{18-20.5-23} cm, ending by working a **wrong** side row.

Bind off all sts **loosely** in ribbing leaving a long end for sewing.

Repeat for second Sleeve.

FINISHING
NECK RIBBING

With **right** side facing and using smaller size needle, knit 4{5-5-5} sts from Right Front st holder, pick up 16{18-20-22} sts evenly spaced along Right Neck edge, slip 14{16-16-16} sts from Back st holder onto empty needle and knit across, pick up 16{18-20-22} sts evenly spaced along Left Neck edge, slip 4{5-5-5} sts from st holder onto empty needle and knit across: 54{62-66-70} sts.

Row 1: P2, (K2, P2) across.

Row 2: K2, (P2, K2) across.

Repeat Rows 1 and 2 until Ribbing measures approximately 1" (2.5 cm), ending by working a **wrong** side row.

Bind off all sts in ribbing.

FRONT EDGING

With **right** side facing and using smaller size needle, pick up and knit 54{58-62-64} sts evenly spaced along Front edge and Neck Ribbing, leaving Bottom Ribbing unworked.

Row 1: Knit across.

Bind off all sts in **knit**.

Repeat for second edge.

Weave underarm and side in one continuous seam **(Fig. 15, page 78)**.

Sew zipper in place, beginning 1" (2.5 cm) from the bottom edge and adjusting top of zipper as needed.

Sew 2 buttons to Left Front opposite buttonholes.

Design by Dorothy Ratigan.

Note: Jacket width includes 2 edge stitches.

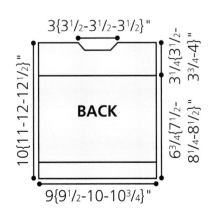

BACK

3{3½-3½-3½}"

10{11-12-12½}"

3¼{3½-3¾-4}"

6¾{7½-8-8½}"

9{9½-10-10¾}"

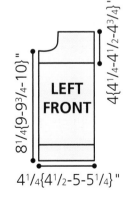

LEFT FRONT

4{4¼-4½-4¾}"

8¼{9-9¾-10}"

4¼{4½-5-5¼}"

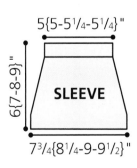

SLEEVE

5{5-5¼-5¼}"

6{7-8-9}"

7¾{8¼-9-9½}"

tote

◼◼◻◻ EASY

Finished Size: 15³/₄" (40 cm) at bottom x 12" (30.5 cm) at top x 10" (25.5 cm) high

MATERIALS
Deborah Norville Collection, Serenity Chunky Weight Yarn 🔵**5**
[3.5 ounces, 109 yards (100 grams, 100 meters) per skein]:
  Color A #13 Forest - 2 skeins
  Color B #01 Almond - 1 skein
Straight knitting needles, size 9 (5.5 mm) **or** size needed for gauge
Yarn needle
³/₄" (19 mm) Buttons - 4
Sewing needle and thread
Fabric for lining (optional)

♦**GAUGE:** In Seed Stitch, 13 sts and 26 rows = 4" (10 cm)

SIDE (Make 2)
With Color A, cast on 53 sts.

Rows 1-7: K1, (P1, K1) across.

Row 8 (Right side - Decrease row)**:** SSK *(Figs. 9a-c, page 75)*, K1, (P1, K1) across to last 2 sts, K2 tog *(Fig. 8, page 75)*; drop Color A: 51 sts.

Carry unused yarn on **wrong** side, twisting yarns every other row.

Rows 9-13: With Color B, P1, (K1, P1) across.

Row 14 (Decrease row)**:** SSK, P1, (K1, P1) across to last 2 sts, K2 tog; drop Color B: 49 sts.

Rows 15-42: Beginning with Color A, repeat Rows 1-14 twice: 41 sts

Rows 43-50: With Color A, K1, (P1, K1) across.

Rows 51-56: With Color B, K1, (P1, K1) across.

Two colors of Serenity Chunky Weight Yarn alternate to create the striped body of this roomy tote. Since the yarn is variegated, using just one color will also yield stripes with less contrast. The handles are wide and sturdy, while the fabric lining adds more stability.

*We've all gone green…but now, with this easy-to-knit bag, you can be green **and** stylish!*

—Deborah

Rows 57-64: With Color A, K1, (P1, K1) across.

Bind off all sts in pattern leaving a long end for sewing on one piece only.

Sew sides and bottom seam.

HANDLE (Make 2)

With Color A, cast on 97 sts.

Rows 1-8: K1, (P1, K1) across.

Bind off all sts in pattern.

Line Tote and wrong side of Handles if desired.

Using photo as a guide for placement and placing a button on top of each end of each Handle, sew buttons and Handles to top edge of Tote.

stockings

Finished Size: 8 " x 26 " (20.5 cm x 66 cm)

Christmas is sure to be more fun when your stocking holds twice as much! These oversized designs are both made from one pattern. The stripes on the green stocking are knitted at random, while the Santa face on the red stocking can be knit in or added with easy Duplicate Stitch.

MATERIALS

Deborah Norville Collection, Serenity Worsted Weight Yarn **MEDIUM 4**
[3.5 ounces, 186 yards (100 grams, 170 meters) per skein]:
Santa
Main Color #16 Christmas Red - 2 skeins
Contrasting Color #01 White - 1 skein
#52 Black or embroidery floss - small amount for eyebrows
Stripes
Main Color #34 Green - 1 skein
Contrasting Colors #01 White and #16 Christmas Red - 1 skein
   each
Straight knitting needles, size 9 (5.5 mm) **or** size needed for gauge
Stitch holders - 3
Markers
Yarn needle

♦**GAUGE:** In Stockinette Stitch, 18 sts and 23 rows = 4 " (10 cm)

RIBBING

With Main Color and leaving a long end for sewing, cast on 74 sts.

Work in K1, P1 ribbing for 2 " (5 cm).

LEG

SANTA STOCKING

The Santa design can be knit in as you go or duplicate stitched after you finish knitting and before you sew the seam. We used duplicate stitch on our model.

Duplicate Stitch Version:
Work in Stockinette Stitch (knit one row, purl one row) until Leg measures approximately 16" (40.5 cm) from cast on edge, ending by working a **knit** row.

Knit-in Version: Work in Stockinette Stitch for 3¾" (9.5 cm), ending by working a **purl** row.

Santa Row 1: K3, place marker **(see Markers, page 70)**; follow Row 1 of chart on page 57 across 32 sts **(see Following a Chart, page 76 and Changing Colors, page 77)**; place marker, knit across.

Follow chart through Row 37, then use Main Color until Leg measures approximately 16" (40.5 cm) from cast on edge, ending by working a **knit** row.

STRIPED STOCKING

Changing colors as desired, work in Stockinette Stitch (knit one row, purl one row) until Leg measures approximately 16" (40.5 cm) from cast on edge, ending by working a **knit** row.

Instructions continue on page 56.

My mother knitted the Christmas stocking that I STILL hang every year. And I've knitted the stockings that MY children hang. Start your own family's tradition with this stocking. (And don't forget to put a bell on the toe so you hear when Santa's putting the toys in!)

— Deborah

LEFT HEEL

When instructed to slip a stitch, always slip as if to **purl** with yarn held to **wrong** side, unless otherwise instructed.

Use Main Color for both Stockings.

Dividing Stitches: P 14, slip next 46 sts onto st holder (top of Foot), slip last 14 sts onto second st holder (Right Heel): 14 sts.

Row 1: Slip 1, knit across.

Row 2: Purl across.

Rows 3-17: Repeat Rows 1 and 2, 7 times; then repeat Row 1 once **more**.

TURNING HEEL

Begin working short rows as follows:

Row 1: P2, P2 tog **(Fig. 11, page 76)**, P1, leave remaining 9 sts unworked; **turn**.

Row 2: Slip 1, K3: 13 sts.

Row 3: P3, P2 tog, P1, leave remaining 7 sts unworked; turn.

Row 4: Slip 1, K4: 12 sts.

Row 5: P4, P2 tog, P1, leave remaining 5 sts unworked; turn.

Row 6: Slip 1, K5: 11 sts.

Row 7: P5, P2 tog, P1, leave remaining 3 sts unworked; turn.

Row 8: Slip 1, K6: 10 sts.

Row 9: P6, P2 tog, P1, leave remaining st unworked; turn.

Row 10: Slip 1, K7: 9 sts.

Row 11: P7, P2 tog: 8 sts.

Slip remaining sts onto st holder; cut yarn.

RIGHT HEEL

With **wrong** side facing, slip 14 sts from Right Heel st holder onto needle.

Use Main Color for both Stockings.

Row 1: Slip 1, purl across.

Row 2: Knit across.

Rows 3-17: Repeat Rows 1 and 2, 7 times; then repeat Row 1 once **more**.

TURNING HEEL

Begin working short rows as follows:

Row 1: K2, SSK **(Figs. 9a-c, page 75)**, K1, leave remaining 9 sts unworked; **turn**.

Row 2: Slip 1, P3: 13 sts.

Row 3: K3, SSK, K1, leave remaining 7 sts unworked; turn.

Row 4: Slip 1, P4: 12 sts.

Row 5: K4, SSK, K1, leave remaining 5 sts unworked; turn.

Row 6: Slip 1, P5: 11 sts.

Row 7: K5, SSK, K1, leave remaining 3 sts unworked; turn.

Row 8: Slip 1, P6: 10 sts.

Row 9: K6, SSK, K1, leave remaining st unworked; turn.

Row 10: Slip 1, P7: 9 sts.

Row 11: K7, SSK; do **not** cut yarn: 8 sts.

GUSSET

For Striped Stocking, change colors as desired.

Row 1: With **right** side facing, pick up and knit 9 sts along side of Right Heel **(Fig. 17a, page 79)**, place marker **(see Markers, page 70)**, knit across top of Foot st holder, place marker, pick up and knit 9 sts along side of Left Heel, slip 8 sts from Left Heel st holder onto empty needle and knit across: 80 sts.

Row 2: Purl across.

Row 3 (Decrease row): Knit across to within 2 sts of next marker, K2 tog **(Fig. 8, page 75)**, knit across to next marker, SSK, knit across: 78 sts.

Rows 4-13: Repeat Rows 2 and 3, 5 times: 68 sts.

Remove markers.

FOOT

For Striped Stocking, continue to change colors as desired.

Beginning with a **purl** row, work in Stockinette Stitch for 4" (10 cm), ending by working a purl row.

TOE

Use Main Color for both Stockings.

Row 1 (Decrease row): K 15, K2 tog, place marker, K1, SSK, K 28, K2 tog, place marker, K1, SSK, knit across: 64 sts.

Row 2: Purl across.

Row 3 (Decrease row): ★ Knit across to within 2 sts of next marker, K2 tog, K1, SSK; repeat from ★ once **more**, knit across: 60 sts.

Rows 4-17: Repeat Rows 2 and 3, 7 times: 32 sts.

Row 18: Purl across removing markers.

Row 19: K2 tog across: 16 sts.

Bind off all sts in **purl**.

KEY
□ - Red
▨ - White
╱ - Black Backstitch
╱ - Red Backstitch

DUPLICATE STITCH SANTA

Read about Duplicate Stitch **(Figs. 14a & b, page 77)**. Each square on the chart below represents one stitch. The key indicates color of yarn to use. Begin the design with Row 1 and work up the chart. Chart will be placed 3 sts from the right edge as you hold the Stocking with ribbing at bottom. Begin bottom of chart (top of Santa) 3³/₄" (9.5 cm) from the ribbing and across 32 sts and 37 rows.

Following chart for placement, first work all of the Duplicate Stitches and then work backstitch to outline face **(Fig. 19, page 80)**.

FINISHING

Using long yarn end, weave back seam **(Fig. 15, page 78)**; join bound off sts on Toe **(Figs. 16a & b, page 78)**.

HANGING LOOP

With Main Color, cast on 24 sts.

Bind off all sts in **knit** leaving a long end for sewing Hanging Loop.

Sew Hanging Loop at inside of Cuff at seam.

The Stocking is worked from the top down; follow the chart beginning at the top of Santa's head.

SANTA CHART

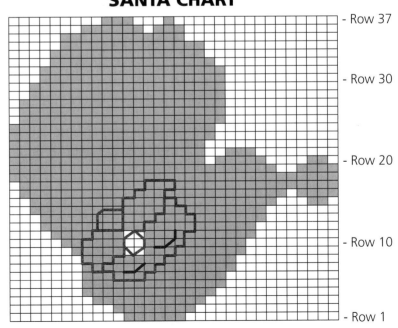

- Row 37
- Row 30
- Row 20
- Row 10
- Row 1

Note: On **right** side rows, follow chart from **right** to **left**.
On **wrong** side rows, follow chart from **left** to **right**.

bears

◖■□□ EASY

Finished Size: Size will vary depending on the yarn and gauge you choose. The following sizes are approximate:

Sock Weight yarn: 7" (18 cm) tall
Sport Weight yarn: 9½" (24 cm) tall
Worsted Weight yarn: 12" (30.5 cm) tall
Chunky Weight yarn: 16" (40.5 cm) tall

MATERIALS

Deborah Norville Collection, Serenity Sock Weight Yarn **SUPER FINE 1**
[1.76 ounces, 230 yards (50 grams, 210 meters) per skein]:
#04-03 Cinnamon - 2 skeins
Straight knitting needles, size 2 (2.75 mm)

Deborah Norville Collection, Serenity Sport Weight Yarn **FINE 2**
[3.5 ounces, 361 yards (100 grams, 330 meters) per skein]:
#48 Heather Grey - 1 skein
Straight knitting needles, size 4 (3.5 mm)

Deborah Norville Collection, Serenity Worsted Weight Yarn (Panda) **ME**
[3.5 ounces, 186 yards (100 grams, 170 meters) per skein]:
#01 White and #52 Black - 1 skein **each**
Straight knitting needles, size 7 (4.5 mm)

Deborah Norville Collection, Serenity Chunky Weight Yarn **BULKY 5**
[3.5 ounces, 109 yards (100 grams, 100 meters) per skein]:
#16 Chocolate - 2 skeins
Straight knitting needles, size 9 (5.5 mm)

Markers
Tapestry or Yarn needle
Sewing needle and thread
Polyester fiberfill
Felt for eyes and nose

Note: Listed are the needle sizes we used to insure the fiberfill would not show through the knitted fabric. You may need to experiment depending on your personal tension.

With Serenity Yarns from the Deborah Norville Collection, you can be a toymaker extraordinaire! From left to right in the photo, these bears were made using Sock Weight, Worsted Weight, Chunky Weight, and Sport Weight Yarns. All the bears were made from the same pattern, with color variations for the panda.

Instructions continue on page 60.

We did these up in "real" bear colors, but how about a bear family to match your child's room? It's sure to be the new favorite toy that gets snuggled every night.

—Deborah

LEGS

Note: Both Legs will be worked at the same time using separate yarn for each Leg. For the Panda Bear, use Black.

Leaving a long end for sewing, cast on 5 sts; with second yarn, cast on 5 sts.

The increases that are used in this pattern are made by knitting into the front **and** into the back of one stitch **(Figs. 4a & b, page 74)**.

Row 1: Increase in each st across: 10 sts **each** Leg.

Row 2: Knit across.

Row 3: Increase in each st across: 20 sts **each** Leg.

Rows 4-34: Knit across.

BODY

Note: For the Panda Bear, continue using Black for Row 1, then change to White for remaining rows.

Row 1 (Joining row - Right side)**:** Knit across both Legs with first yarn; cut second yarn: 40 sts.

Rows 2-20: Knit across.

For the Panda Bear, change to Black.

Row 21 (Decrease row)**:** K8, K2 tog **(Fig. 8, page 75)**, place marker **(see Markers, page 70)**, SSK **(Figs. 9a-c, page 75)**, K 16, K2 tog, place marker, SSK, K8: 36 sts.

Rows 22-24: Knit across.

Row 25 (Decrease row)**:** ★ Knit across to within 2 sts of next marker, K2 tog, SSK; repeat from ★ once **more**, knit across: 32 sts.

Rows 26-37: Repeat Rows 22-25, 3 times: 20 sts.

Rows 38-42: Knit across.

Leave markers in place.

SOLID HEAD

Row 1: K4, increase twice, K3, increase, place marker for nose, increase, K3, increase twice, K4: 26 sts.

Row 2: Knit across.

Row 3 (Increase row)**:** (Knit across to within one st of next marker, increase twice) 3 times, knit across: 32 sts.

Row 4: Knit across.

Rows 5-10: Repeat Rows 3 and 4, 3 times: 50 sts.

Row 11 (Decrease row)**:** Knit across to within 2 sts of second marker, K2 tog, SSK, knit across: 48 sts.

Row 12: Knit across.

Rows 13-20: Repeat Rows 11 and 12, 4 times: 40 sts.

Row 21: Knit across to within 2 sts of first marker, K2 tog, SSK, removing marker for nose, knit across to within 2 sts of last marker, K2 tog, SSK, knit across: 36 sts.

Row 22: Knit across.

Row 23 (Decrease row): ★ Knit across to within 2 sts of next marker, K2 tog, SSK; repeat from ★ once **more**, knit across: 32 sts.

Row 24: Knit across.

Rows 25-30: Repeat Rows 23 and 24, 3 times: 20 sts.

Bind off all sts in **knit**.

PANDA HEAD
Row 1: Cut Black; using White, K4, increase twice, K3, increase, place marker for nose, increase, K3, increase twice, K4: 26 sts.

Row 2: Knit across.

Row 3 (Increase row): (Knit across to within one st of next marker, increase twice) 3 times, knit across: 32 sts.

Row 4: Knit across.

Rows 5-10: Repeat Rows 3 and 4, 3 times: 50 sts.

Cut 2 strands of Black yarn, each 40" (101.5 cm) long to be used for the eye patches.

Twist the yarns when changing colors to prevent holes and carry the White yarn **loosely** on the wrong side *(Figs. 13a & b, page 77)*.

Row 11: Knit across to first marker, K5, with Black K3, with White K5, K2 tog, SSK, K5, with Black K3, with White knit across: 48 sts.

Row 12: Knit across working the White sts with White and the Black sts with Black.

Row 13: Knit across to first marker, K5, with Black K4, with White K3, K2 tog, SSK, K3, with Black K4, with White knit across: 46 sts.

Row 14: Knit across working the White sts with White and the Black sts with Black.

Row 15: Knit across to first marker, K5, with Black K5, with White K1, K2 tog, SSK, K1, with Black K5, with White knit across: 44 sts.

Row 16: Knit across working the White sts with White and the Black sts with Black.

Row 17: Knit across to first marker, K4, increase, with Black SSK, K1, K2 tog, with White K4, with Black SSK, K1, K2 tog, with White increase, knit across: 42 sts.

Row 18: Knit across working the White sts with White and the Black sts with Black; cut Black.

Row 19: Knit across to within 2 sts of second marker, K2 tog, SSK, knit across: 40 sts.

Row 20: Knit across.

Row 21: Knit across to within 2 sts of first marker, K2 tog, SSK, removing marker for nose, knit across to within 2 sts of last marker, K2 tog, SSK, knit across: 36 sts.

Row 22: Knit across.

Row 23 (Decrease row): ★ Knit across to within 2 sts of next marker, K2 tog, SSK; repeat from ★ once **more**, knit across: 32 sts.

Row 24: Knit across.

Rows 25-30: Repeat Rows 23 and 24, 3 times: 20 sts.

Bind off all sts in **knit**.

Instructions continue on page 62.

ARM (Make 2)

For the Panda Bear, use Black.

Leaving a long end for sewing, cast on 5 sts.

Row 1: Increase in each st across: 10 sts.

Row 2: Knit across.

Row 3: Increase in each st across: 20 sts.

Rows 4-34: Knit across.

Bind off all sts in **knit**.

EAR (Make 2)

For the Panda Bear, use Black.

Leaving a long end for sewing, cast on 10 sts.

Row 1: Increase in each st across: 20 sts.

Rows 2-4: Knit across.

Row 5: K3, K2 tog, SSK, K6, K2 tog, SSK, K3: 16 sts.

Row 6: Knit across.

Row 7: K2, K2 tog, SSK, K4, K2 tog, SSK, K2: 12 sts.

Row 8: Knit across.

Bind off all sts in **knit**.

ASSEMBLY

Thread tapestry or yarn needle with yarn end on Leg and weave through cast on sts, pull tightly and secure; sew Leg seam. Stuff Leg with polyester fiberfill.

Flatten Leg at Joining Row with seam to inside. Working through **both** thicknesses, sew across Joining Row.

Repeat for second Leg.

Sew back seam on Body.

Stuff Body with polyester fiberfill. Continue to sew back seam on Head, shaping muzzle area as you go.

Join bound off sts at top of Head **(Figs. 16a & b, page 78)**, adding additional stuffing before closing.

Thread tapestry or yarn needle with yarn end on Arm and weave through cast on sts, pull tightly and secure; sew Arm seam. Stuff Arm with polyester fiberfill. Using photo as a guide for placement, sew Arm to Body.

Repeat for second Arm.

Sew end of rows of Ear together for back seam; then join bound off sts for top seam. Sew Ear to top of Head, beginning at corner of top seam on Head.

Repeat for second Ear.

Cut one circle of contrasting color felt for each eye and an oval for the nose. Using photo as a guide for placement and using sewing needle and thread, sew eyes and nose in place.

Design by Evelyn A. Clark.

media holders

*What a great gift idea! My sons have commissioned these a number of times! I've done their school colors, initials and now I **know** my little girl is going to ask for that yummy white heart!*

—*Deborah*

Need quick and easy gifts for teens and preteens? These little drawstring media holders will make a personal statement. The icons can be knit into the holder, or added with Duplicate Stitch.

Instructions begin on page 64.

Finished Size: 3" (7.5 cm) wide x 5¾" (14.5 cm) high

MATERIALS
Deborah Norville Collection, Serenity Sport Weight Yarn **FINE 2**
[3.5 ounces, 361 yards (100 grams, 330 meters) per skein]:
Heart
Main Color #17 Fuchsia - 1 skein
Contrasting Color #01 White - 1 skein
Flower
Main Color #34 Green - 1 skein
Contrasting Color #07 Peach - 1 skein
Peace Sign
Main Color #45 Chocolate Brown - 1 skein
Contrasting Color #04 Canary - 1 skein
Skull
Main Color #52 Black - 1 skein
Contrasting Color #01 White - 1 skein
Straight knitting needles, size 3 (3.25 mm) **or** size needed for gauge
Double pointed needles (for Cord), size 3 (3.25 cm)
Split-ring markers (if knitting from a chart)
Tapestry needle
Button or bead for Flower center

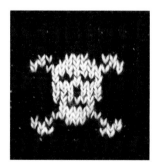

♦**GAUGE:** In Stockinette Stitch, 13 sts and 16 rows = 2" (5 cm)

HOLDER
KNIT-IN VERSION
Cast on 43 sts.

Knit 8 rows (Garter Stitch Band).

Work 1" of Stockinette Stitch (purl one row, knit one row).

Begin following the chart on a **right** side row **(see Following a Chart, page 76 and Changing Colors, page 77)**. Place a marker after the first 15 sts and after the next 13 sts to indicate placement of chart (for peace sign, place second marker after the next 14 sts) **(see Markers, page 70)**.

Work in Stockinette Stitch until piece measures approximately 5" (12.5 cm) from cast on edge, ending by working a **purl** row.

Eyelet Row (Creates opening for cord): K3, YO *(Fig. 3a, page 73)*, K2 tog *(Fig. 8, page 75)*, (K1, YO, K2 tog) across to last 2 sts, K2.

Purl one row.

Knit last 4 rows.

Bind off all sts in **knit** leaving a long end for sewing.

DUPLICATE STITCH VERSION
Cast on 43 sts.

Knit 8 rows (Garter Stitch Band).

Beginning with a **purl** row, work in Stockinette Stitch (purl one row, knit one row) until piece measures approximately 5" (12.5 cm) from cast on edge, ending by working a **purl** row.

Eyelet Row (Creates opening for cord): K3, YO *(Fig. 3a, page 73)*, K2 tog *(Fig. 8, page 75)*, (K1, YO, K2 tog) across to last 2 sts, K2.

Purl one row.

Knit last 4 rows.

Bind off all sts in **knit** leaving a long end for sewing.

Duplicate Stitch desired icon by following chart *(Figs. 14a & b, page 77)*.

Center the chart on the Holder, beginning 1" (2.5 cm) from Garter Stitch Band, and skipping 15 sts from the right edge.

FINISHING
Sew one or two buttons stacked to the center of the flower.

Weave end of rows together for back seam *(Fig. 15, page 78)*.

Fold cast on edge flat, placing seam at center; sew bottom seam.

CORD
Using double pointed needle and Contrasting Color, cast on 3 sts.

Without turning, slide the sts to the opposite end of the needle. Pull the working yarn across the back and knit across.

Now slide the work again, give the cord end a tug, pull the yarn across the back and knit across.

Note: Add some tension when knitting the first stitch, so the working yarn is pulled tight, joining the first and last stitches together. It is also helpful to give the Cord a tug after each row.

Repeat this process until the Cord is approximately 12" (30.5 cm) long **or** desired length.

Bind off all sts in **knit** leaving a long end for sewing.

Weave Cord through Eyelet Row. Sew ends of Cord together.

HEART CHART
■ - Main Color
□ - Contrasting Color

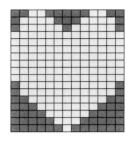

FLOWER CHART
■ - Main Color
■ - Contrasting Color

PEACE SIGN CHART
■ - Main Color
□ - Contrasting Color

SKULL CHART
■ - Main Color
□ - Contrasting Color

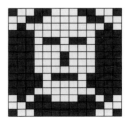

CHUNKY YARN

Serenity Chunky Weight Yarn is Deborah's favorite yarn in the Serenity line. Twenty novel prints in beautiful color combinations keep your stitching interesting, and since the yarn is chunky, you'll finish your projects quickly.

BULKY 5

100% fine acrylic
3.5 ounces/100 grams; 109 yards/100 meters

Machine wash, warm; tumble dry on low.

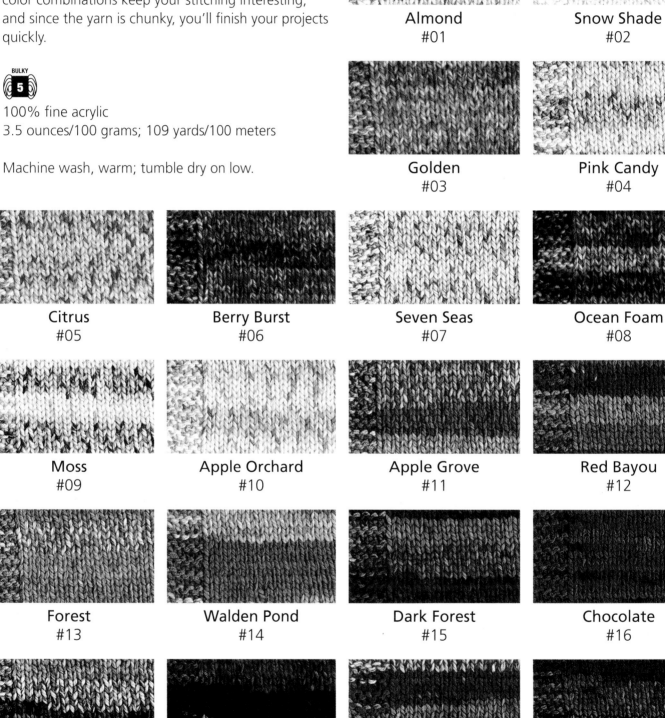

Almond
#01

Snow Shade
#02

Golden
#03

Pink Candy
#04

Citrus
#05

Berry Burst
#06

Seven Seas
#07

Ocean Foam
#08

Moss
#09

Apple Orchard
#10

Apple Grove
#11

Red Bayou
#12

Forest
#13

Walden Pond
#14

Dark Forest
#15

Chocolate
#16

Memphis Blues
#17

Stormy
#18

Christmas
#19

America
#20

SOCK YARN

Serenity Sock Weight Yarn is a combination of superwash Merino wool, nylon and soft bamboo, and is available in 18 colorways. Projects made with this yarn maintain their drape and softness through machine washing and drying. Perfect for socks, you'll also love this yarn for shawls, baby blankets and sweaters.

50% superwash Merino wool/25% bamboo/25% nylon
1.76 ounces/50 grams; 230 yards/210 meters

Machine wash, warm; tumble dry on low.

Thyme
#04-01

Mint
#04-02

Cinnamon
#04-03

Purple Spice
#04-04

Paprika
#04-05

Indigo
#04-06

Chili
#04-07

Saffron
#04-08

Lavender Topaz
#08-01

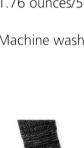
Jasper
#08-02

Picasso Marble
#08-03

Rose Quartz
#08-04

Tanzanite
#08-05

Obsidian
#08-06

Citrine
#08-07

Aquamarine
#08-08

Sapphire
#08-09

Amethyst
#08-10

WORSTED & SPORT YARN

Colors and color numbers are the same for both weight

Serenity Sport Weight Yarn is unbelievably soft, thanks to a blend of super-fine acrylic and nylon. The lighter weight is just right for baby and toddler projects; and with 52 solid shades to choose from, you'll always be able to find the color you need.

FINE 2

55% super-fine nylon/45% super-fine acrylic
3.5 ounces/100 grams; 361 yards/330 meters

Machine wash, warm; tumble dry on low.

Serenity Worsted Weight Yarn is a multipurpose acrylic/nylon yarn for fashion sweaters, stylish accessories, comfy afghans and cozy home décor. The wide range of 52 solid colors includes fashion shades and hues that will look right at home in your home.

MEDIUM 4

55% super-fine nylon/45% super-fine acrylic
3.5 ounces/100 grams; 186 yards/170 meters

Machine wash, warm; tumble dry on low.

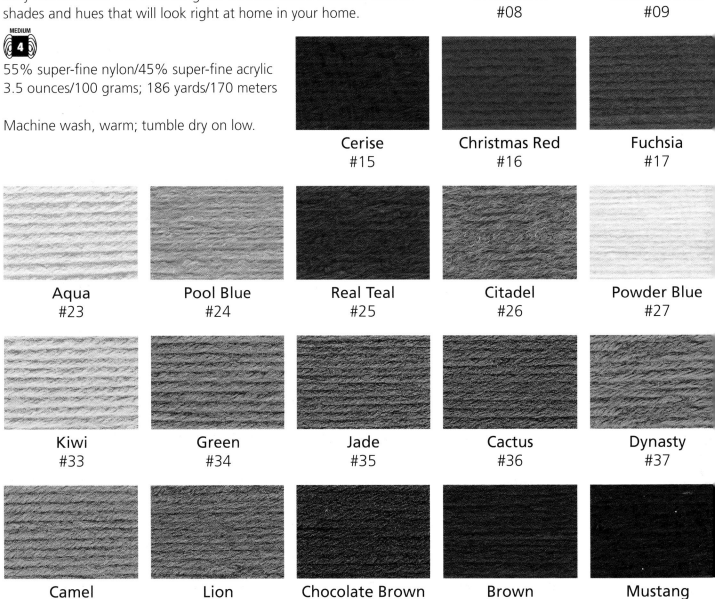

White
#01

Ivory
#02

Grenadine
#08

Rustic Brown
#09

Cerise
#15

Christmas Red
#16

Fuchsia
#17

Aqua
#23

Pool Blue
#24

Real Teal
#25

Citadel
#26

Powder Blue
#27

Kiwi
#33

Green
#34

Jade
#35

Cactus
#36

Dynasty
#37

Camel
#43

Lion
#44

Chocolate Brown
#45

Brown
#46

Mustang
#47

KNIT WITH DEBORAH NORVILLE

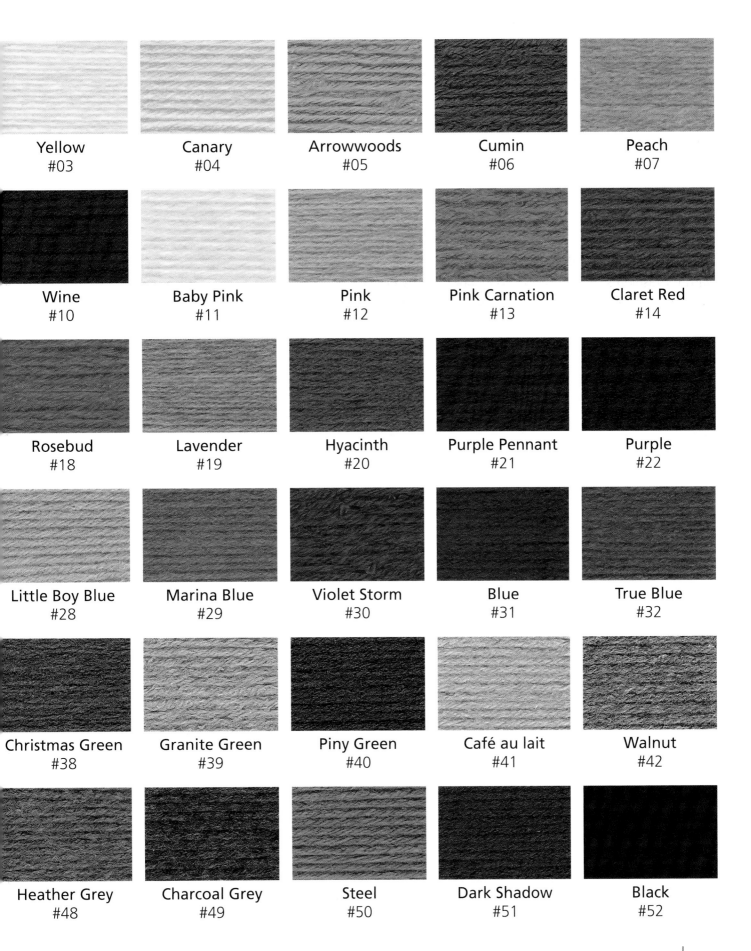

Yellow #03	Canary #04	Arrowwoods #05	Cumin #06	Peach #07
Wine #10	Baby Pink #11	Pink #12	Pink Carnation #13	Claret Red #14
Rosebud #18	Lavender #19	Hyacinth #20	Purple Pennant #21	Purple #22
Little Boy Blue #28	Marina Blue #29	Violet Storm #30	Blue #31	True Blue #32
Christmas Green #38	Granite Green #39	Piny Green #40	Café au lait #41	Walnut #42
Heather Grey #48	Charcoal Grey #49	Steel #50	Dark Shadow #51	Black #52

For me knitting has always been therapeutic. Turns out researchers have PROVEN its healthful effects in lowering blood pressure and heart rate.

— *Deborah*

ABBREVIATIONS

cm	centimeters
K	knit
mm	millimeters
P	purl
PSSO	pass slipped stitch over
Rnd(s)	Round(s)
SSK	slip, slip, knit
SSP	slip, slip, purl
st(s)	stitch(es)
tog	together
YO	yarn over

★ — work instructions following ★ as many **more** times as indicated in addition to the first time.

† to † — work all instructions from first † to second † **as many** times as specified.

( ) or **[ ]** — work enclosed instructions **as many** times as specified by the number immediately following **or** contains explanatory remarks.

colon (:) — the number(s) given after a colon at the end of a row or round denote(s) the number of stitches you should have on that row or round.

work even — work without increasing or decreasing in the established pattern.

GAUGE

Exact gauge is **essential** for proper size or fit. Before beginning your project, make a sample swatch in the yarn and needle specified in the individual instructions. After completing the swatch, measure it, counting your stitches and rows carefully. If your swatch is larger or smaller than specified, **make another, changing needle size to get the correct gauge**. Keep trying until you find the size needles that will give you the specified gauge.

MARKERS

As a convenience to you, we have used markers to mark the beginning of a round, to help distinguish the beginning of a pattern, or to mark placement of increases and decreases. Place markers as instructed. You may use purchased markers or tie a length of contrasting color yarn around the needle. When you reach a marker on each row or round, slip it from the left needle to the right needle; remove it when no longer needed. When using double pointed needles, a split-ring marker can be placed around the first stitch in the round to indicate the beginning of the round. Move it up at the end of each round.

ZEROS

To consolidate the length of an involved pattern, Zeros are sometimes used so that all sizes can be combined. For example, (P2, K2) 0{1-2-1} time(s) means that the first size would do nothing, the second and fourth size would work the instructions in the parenthesis once and the third size would work it twice.

KNITTING NEEDLES		
UNITED STATES	ENGLISH U.K.	METRIC (mm)
0	13	2
1	12	2.25
2	11	2.75
3	10	3.25
4	9	3.5
5	8	3.75
6	7	4
7	6	4.5
8	5	5
9	4	5.5
10	3	6
10½	2	6.5
11	1	8
13	00	9
15	000	10
17	---	12.75

KNIT TERMINOLOGY	
UNITED STATES	INTERNATIONAL
gauge =	tension
bind off =	cast off
yarn over (YO) =	yarn forward (yfwd) **or** yarn around needle (yrn)

Yarn Weight Symbol & Names	LACE 0	SUPER FINE 1	FINE 2	LIGHT 3	MEDIUM 4	BULKY 5	SUPER BULKY 6
Type of Yarns in Category	Fingering, size 10 crochet thread	Sock, Fingering, Baby	Sport, Baby	DK, Light Worsted	Worsted, Afghan, Aran	Chunky, Craft, Rug	Bulky, Roving
Knit Gauge Range* in Stockinette St to 4" (10 cm)	33-40** sts	27-32 sts	23-26 sts	21-24 sts	16-20 sts	12-15 sts	6-11 sts
Advised Needle Size Range	000-1	1 to 3	3 to 5	5 to 7	7 to 9	9 to 11	11 and larger

*GUIDELINES ONLY: The chart above reflects the most commonly used gauges and needle sizes for specific yarn categories.

** Lace weight yarns are usually knitted on larger needles to create lacy openwork patterns. Accordingly, a gauge range is difficult to determine. Always follow the gauge stated in your pattern.

■□□□ BEGINNER	Projects for first-time knitters using basic knit and purl stitches. Minimal shaping.
■■□□ EASY	Projects using basic stitches, repetitive stitch patterns, simple color changes, and simple shaping and finishing.
■■■□ INTERMEDIATE	Projects with a variety of stitches, such as basic cables and lace, simple intarsia, double-pointed needles and knitting in the round needle techniques, mid-level shaping and finishing.
■■■■ EXPERIENCED	Projects using advanced techniques and stitches, such as short rows, fair isle, more intricate intarsia, cables, lace patterns, and numerous color changes.

USING DOUBLE POINTED NEEDLES

When working too few stitches to use a circular needle, as for the Mittens and Socks, double pointed needles are required. The **Mittens** are worked on three needles. Dividing the stitches into thirds, slip one-third of the stitches onto each of 3 double pointed needles **(Fig. 1a)**, forming a triangle.

Fig. 1a

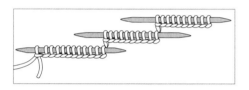

The **Socks** are worked on four needles. Divide the stitches as specified in the instructions forming a square **(Fig. 1b)**.

Fig. 1b

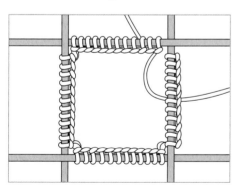

With the working yarn coming from the stitch on the last needle and using the remaining needle, work across the stitches on the first needle being careful to not twist stitches around the needle **(Fig. 1c)**.

Fig. 1c

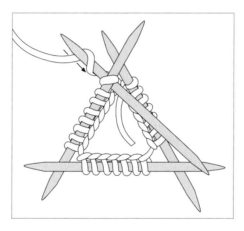

You will now have an empty needle with which to work the stitches from the next needle. Work the first stitch of each needle firmly to prevent gaps. Continue working around without turning the work.

ADDING STITCHES

Insert the right needle into the stitch as if to **knit**, yarn over and pull loop through **(Fig. 2a)**, insert left needle into loop just worked from **front** to **back** and slip it onto the left needle **(Fig. 2b)**. Repeat for the required number of stitches.

Fig. 2a

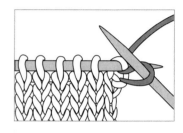

Fig. 2b

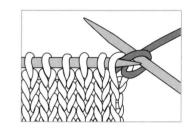

YARN OVERS

A yarn over *(abbreviated YO)* is simply placing the yarn over the right needle creating a new stitch. Since the yarn over produces a hole in the knit fabric, it is used for a lacy effect. On the row following a yarn over, you must be careful to keep it on the needle and treat it as a stitch by knitting or purling it as instructed.

To make a yarn over, you'll loop the yarn over the needle like you would to knit or purl a stitch, bringing it either to the front or the back of the piece so that it'll be ready to work the next stitch, creating a new stitch on the needle as follows:

After a knit stitch, before a knit stitch

Bring the yarn forward **between** the needles, then back **over** the top of the right hand needle, so that it is now in position to knit the next stitch *(Fig. 3a)*.

Fig. 3a

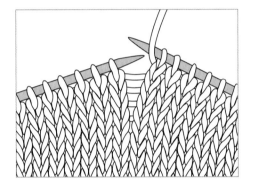

After a purl stitch, before a purl stitch

Bring the yarn **over** the top of the right hand needle to the back, then forward **under** it, so that it is now in position to purl the next stitch *(Fig. 3b)*.

Fig. 3b

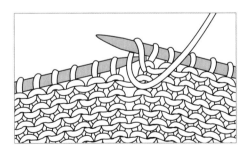

After a knit stitch, before a purl stitch

Bring the yarn forward **between** the needles, then back **over** the top of the right hand needle and forward **between** the needles again, so that it is now in position to purl the next stitch *(Fig. 3c)*.

Fig. 3c

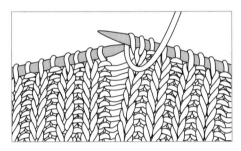

After a purl stitch, before a knit stitch

Bring the yarn **over** the top of the right hand needle to the back, so that it is now in position to knit the next stitch *(Fig. 3d)*.

Fig. 3d

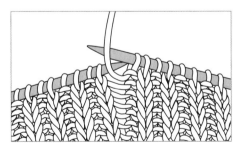

INCREASES

KNIT INCREASE

The knit increase uses one stitch to make two stitches. You will have two stitches on the right needle for the one stitch worked off the left needle.

Knit the next stitch but do **not** slip the old stitch off the left needle **(Fig. 4a)**. Insert the right needle into the **back** loop of the **same** stitch and knit it **(Fig. 4b)**, then slip the old stitch off the left needle.

Fig. 4a

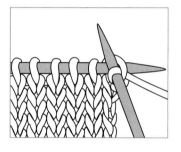

Fig. 4b

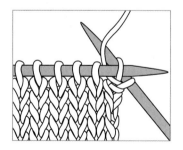

MAKE ONE

Insert the **left** needle under the horizontal strand between the stitches from the front **(Fig. 5a)**. Then knit into the **back** of the strand **(Fig. 5b)**.

Fig. 5a

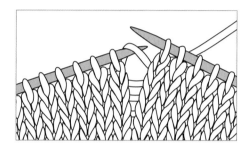

Fig. 5b

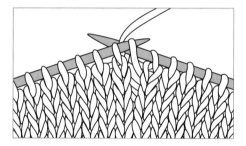

RIGHT INVISIBLE INCREASE

Insert the right needle from the **front** into the side of the stitch **below** the next stitch on the left needle **(Fig. 6)** and knit it.

Fig. 6

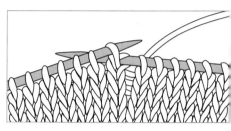

DECREASES

LEFT INVISIBLE INCREASE

Insert the **left** needle from the **back** into the side of the stitch 2 rows **below** the stitch on the right needle *(Fig. 7a)*, pull it up and knit into the **back** loop *(Fig. 7b)*.

Fig. 7a

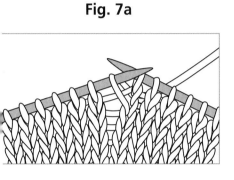

Fig. 7b

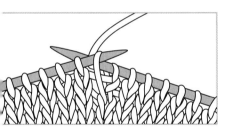

KNIT 2 TOGETHER
(abbreviated K2 tog)

Insert the right needle into the **front** of the first two stitches on the left needle as if to **knit** *(Fig. 8)*, then **knit** them together as if they were one stitch.

Fig. 8

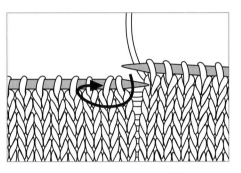

SLIP, SLIP, KNIT
(abbreviated SSK)

Separately slip two stitches as if to **knit** *(Fig. 9a)*. Insert the **left** needle into the **front** of both slipped stitches *(Fig. 9b)* and then **knit** them together as if they were one stitch *(Fig. 9c)*.

Fig. 9a

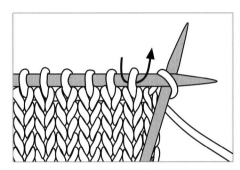

Fig. 9b

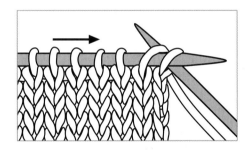

Fig. 9c

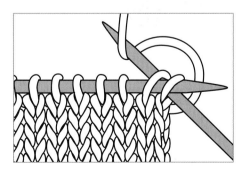

SLIP 1, KNIT 2 TOGETHER, PASS SLIPPED STITCH OVER
(abbreviated slip 1, K2 tog, PSSO)

Slip one stitch as if to **knit** *(Fig. 10a)*, then **knit** the next two stitches together *(Fig. 8, page 75)*. With the left needle, bring the slipped stitch over the stitch just made *(Fig. 10b)* and off the needle.

Fig. 10a

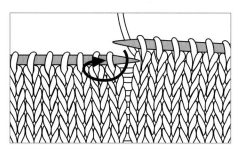

Fig. 10b

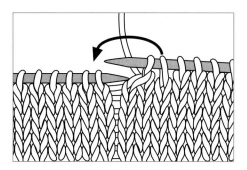

PURL 2 TOGETHER
(abbreviated P2 tog)

Insert the right needle into the **front** of the first two stitches on the left needle as if to **purl** *(Fig. 11)*, then **purl** them together as if they were one stitch.

Fig. 11

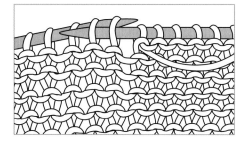

SLIP, SLIP, PURL
(abbreviated SSP)

Separately slip two stitches as if to **knit** *(Fig. 9a, page 75)*. Slip these two stitches back onto the left needle. Insert the **left** needle into the **back** of both stitches from **back** to **front** and then purl them together as if they were one stitch *(Fig. 12)*.

Fig. 12

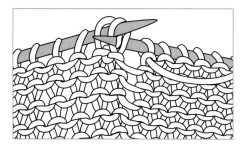

FOLLOWING A CHART

Designs for the Stocking and Media Holder are worked from a chart. It is easier to follow a chart than written instructions and you can also see what the design looks like. The chart shows each stitch as a square indicating what color each stitch should be. Visualize the chart as your fabric, beginning at the bottom edge. If the chart is symmetrical, as in the Media Holders, it doesn't matter which direction the chart is followed.

If the chart is **not** symmetrical, as for the Stocking, work as follows: On **right** side rows, follow the chart from **right** to **left**; on **wrong** side rows, follow the chart from **left** to **right**.

For ease in following the chart, place a ruler on the chart under the row being worked to help keep your place.

CHANGING COLORS

Wind small amounts of each color onto a bobbin to keep the different color yarns from tangling. You'll need one bobbin for each color change, except when there are so few stitches of the new color that it would be easier to carry the unused color **loosely** across the back *(Fig. 13a)*. Always keep the bobbins on the **wrong** side of the piece. When changing colors, always pick up the new color yarn from **beneath** the dropped yarn and keep the color which has just been worked to the left *(Fig. 13b)*. This will prevent holes in the finished piece. Take extra care to keep your tension even. For proper size, it is essential to maintain gauge.

Fig. 13a

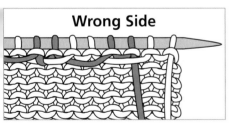

Wrong Side

Fig. 13b

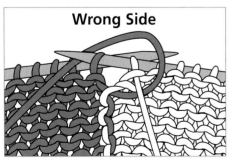

Wrong Side

DUPLICATE STITCH

Duplicate Stitch is worked on Stockinette Stitch. Each knit stitch forms a V and you want to completely cover that V, so that the design appears to have been knit into the piece. Each square on a chart represents one knit stitch that is to be covered by a Duplicate Stitch.

Thread a tapestry or yarn needle with an 18" (45.5 cm) length of yarn. Beginning at lower right of a design and with **right** side facing, bring the needle up from the wrong side at the base of the V, leaving an end to be woven in later (never tie knots). The needle should always go between the strands of yarn. Follow the right side of the V up and insert the needle from right to left under the legs of the V immediately above it, keeping the yarn on top of the stitch *(Fig. 14a)*, and draw through. Follow the left side of the V back down to the base and insert the needle back through the bottom of the same stitch where the first stitch began *(Fig. 14b, Duplicate Stitch completed)*.

Continuing to follow chart, bring the needle up through the next stitch. Repeat for each stitch, keeping your tension the same as the tension of the knit fabric to avoid puckering.

When a length of yarn is finished, run it under several stitches on back of work to secure.

Fig. 14a

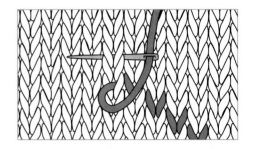

Fig. 14b

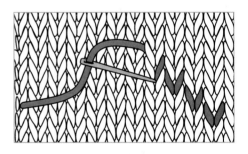

WEAVING SEAMS

With the **right** side of both pieces facing you and edges even, sew through both sides once to secure the beginning of the seam. Insert the needle under the bar **between** the first and second stitches on the row and pull the yarn through **(Fig. 15)**. Insert the needle under the next bar on the second side. Repeat from side to side, being careful to match rows. If the edges are different lengths, it may be necessary to insert the needle under two bars at one edge.

Fig. 15

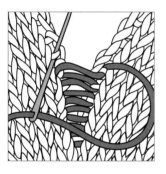

JOINING BOUND OFF STITCHES

Joining bound off stitches can appear seamless. Thread a yarn needle with the long end. With the **right** side of the piece facing you, and matching the top corners, place the bound off stitches together.
Bring the needle from behind the work and through the center of the first stitch. ★ Bring the needle over the top of the bound off sts and pick up both loops of the corresponding stitch on the second side **(Fig. 16a)**. Bring the needle back over the bound off sts and pick up the inverted V of the next stitch **(Fig. 16b)**. Repeat from ★ across. Pull the yarn gently every 2 or 3 stitches, being careful to maintain even tension.

Fig. 16a

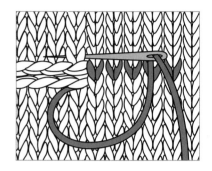

Fig. 16b

PICKING UP STITCHES

When instructed to pick up stitches, insert the needle from the **front** to the **back** under two strands at the edge of the worked piece *(Figs. 17a & b)*. Put the yarn around the needle as if to **knit**, then bring the needle with the yarn back through the stitch to the right side, resulting in a stitch on the needle.

Repeat this along the edge, picking up the required number of stitches.

A crochet hook may be helpful to pull yarn through.

When instructed to **pick up and knit stitches**, pick up a stitch with the right needle and slip it onto the left needle, then knit the stitch. Continue for each stitch to be picked up. This method prevents a ridge on the wrong side.

Fig. 17a

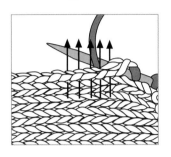

Fig. 17b

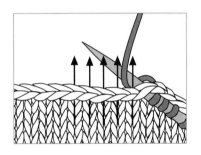

TWISTED CORD

Cut 2 pieces of yarn, each **3 times** longer than the desired finished length. Holding both pieces together, fasten one end to a stationary object **or** have another person hold it; twist until **tight**. Fold it in half and let it twist itself, knot both ends and cut the loops on the folded end.

POM-POM

Cut a piece of cardboard 3" (7.5 cm) wide and as long as you want the diameter of your finished pom-pom to be. Wind the yarn around the cardboard until it is approximately ½" (12 mm) thick in the middle **(Fig. 18a)**. Carefully slip the yarn off the cardboard and firmly tie an 18" (45.5 cm) length of yarn around the middle **(Fig. 18b)**. Leave yarn ends long enough to attach the pom-pom. Cut the loops on both ends and trim the pom-pom into a smooth ball **(Fig.18c)**.

Fig. 18b

Fig. 18c

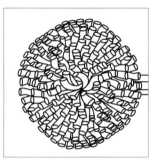

Fig. 18a

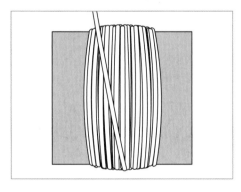

BACKSTITCH

The backstitch is worked from right to left. Come up at 1, go down at 2 and come up at 3 **(Fig. 19)**. The second stitch is made by going down at 1 and coming up at 4.

Fig. 19

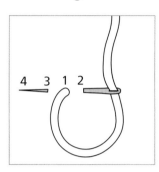